C000085308

My **LIFE** is:
Real vs. Ideal

Proven Practices to Create a Fulfilling Life

Marvin Robert Wohlhueter, Th.D.

WESTBOW
PRESS®
A DIVISION OF THOMAS NELSON
& ZONDERVAN

WestBow Press books may be ordered through booksellers or by contacting:

WestBow Press
A Division of Thomas Nelson & Zondervan
1663 Liberty Drive
Bloomington, IN 47403
www.westbowpress.com
I (866) 928-1240

Author photo provided by Balazs Vizin. To learn more about his offerings as a company, visit his web site or call: *www.cascadecreative.us; Mobile: 470.429.0288*

ISBN: 978-I-9736-6906-7 (sc)
ISBN: 978-I-9736-6907-4 (hc)
ISBN: 978-I-9736-6905-0 (e)

Library of Congress Control Number: 2019909363

Print information available on the last page.

WestBow Press rev. date: 08/27/2019

Dedication

First

My Wife

My *first* book is dedicated to my dear wife, Lorraine, who has encouraged me to write the stories of my heart for the world to read. Her constant love has allowed me to believe in my dreams and in the destiny that God has for my life. Lorraine's adventuresome spirit, shown by moving to America from the Island of Trinidad, has stirred my spirit to soar to new levels of opportunity, enthusiasm, and creativity. Lastly, her commitment to God and her Christ-like character has impacted my life in ways she'll never know this side of Heaven. She has challenged me to become a better man. I am so blessed to share *Life's* journey with her as my Best Friend and Soul Mate. I love you high to the sky! *(As I finish this book, Lorraine is pregnant with twins, a boy and a girl, due in early September, 2019).*

Second

This book is dedicated to Raleigh and Jake. I am reminded every day of the thrill of being your dad. You both have added so much to my life and I am *forever* grateful for you.

Raleigh

You will always be a special daddy's girl and your years of tenderness and care have moved me deeply. I will never forget the *Book of Hope* you made for me during the height of my emotional challenges in 2006. It stirred me to persevere against all odds. Additionally, your *zip-lock bag of change*, given during my joblessness season, warmed my heart *profoundly*. (I still have it over 20 years later.) You would often say as a little girl, "Daddy, why don't you just ask God to send you some happy messengers". You truly believed He would and He did! Your spirited concern for me really cheered me up during those dark years. Thank you for showing me who you really are on the inside! *Today, you are studying to become a Nurse. The world needs your heart of compassion for others.* I love you.

Jake

Every dad would be blessed to have a son like you. We have shared so many good times together as father and son. I remember being your catcher as you learned to pitch at grandma's and grandpa's house. I recall the days when we played street hockey and pretended to be NHL stars. Together, we wrote your fine arts paper while sitting at a Zaxby's restaurant, during a weekend exchange, in Commerce, GA. You won 1st place for telling what being a famous hockey player would be like. Our most extraordinary time together was Father's Day weekend, 2010, when you shared your desire to know God personally and invited Jesus Christ into your heart. We prayed together and cried for joy at your decision. *It was very special to me!* Your attention to detail and your enthusiasm as a junior entrepreneur continues to influence me to grow daily. *Today, you serve in the United States Marine Corp. I am so proud of the man you've become.* Thank you for protecting our freedom. I love you, son!

<u>Most of All</u>

In March 1986, as a 21-year-old, I surrendered my life and heart to Jesus Christ as Savior and Lord. This journey began with passion, intrigue, and deep devotion. I was radically transformed that day from death-to-life and I wanted nothing more than to please God and live for Him each day. Every season of my life has taught me boundless lessons that I would *not* trade for anything. I must confess that it was my faith in God that helped me to *"Embrace My Present Reality"*, then and now. Today, I *celebrate* the person I am becoming because of His amazing grace and unending mercy. I am a work in progress and day-by-day, I see Jesus Christ's imprint on my life.

A BIG Thank You

Every book has as its confession an awareness that others have contributed to bringing it to life. This one is no different! So many people were in my life while the writing was taking place. I am forever grateful to them for their love, support, and interest. These include:

1. *Our Marriage Small Group we lead: Jose and Jennifer, Doug and Nicole, Terry and Johnetta, John and Tammy, Andrew and Tiffany, Eva and Orlando, Mickey and Rhonda, Robin and Mil, Ron and Becky, and Gabe and Kelly.*
2. *Our Marriage Small Group we attend: Dapo and Lara, Gary and Lou, Tony and Ella, and Jim and Lynn.*
3. *My Friday Men's Group I lead (Suwanee, Ga): Jose and Balazs.*
4. *My Friday Men's Group I lead (Cumming, Ga): Scott and Jason.*

Next, Campus Pastor Tim Price and wife, Carey (and Noah, born on May 8, 2019) and the rest of our Free Chapel Cumming family. Your investment into my life along with Lorraine's (and upcoming twins) is *priceless*. We so enjoy doing life together at FCC. To FCC4 (Pastor Tim, Gary, Gabe and myself): Our texted chats on vision, discipleship, and church growth have been exciting and productive. God is shaping a region at FCC. I'm so honored to be a part of the team.

Next, our treasured friends that I would like to mention:

- John and Tammy: John, you have been my Best Friend for almost 4 decades. How does that happen? Your charming family (Tammy and the boys) has been a constant!
- Andrew and Tiffany: Your introduction into our lives while in Greenville, SC was a game-changer for us. We are forever bonded at the heart. We love you, both.
- Chris and Jennifer: Your friendship means the world to Lorraine and me. Thank you for being there for Lorraine's baby shower and the many fanciful baby conversations.

In addition, *Bruce Neill*, I am deeply grateful for your proofing efforts and making this a *better* book. Thank goodness you came along! The world would have witnessed a book with great thought and content, but with errors in grammar, spelling, and flow. Your eye for detail has made this book come alive with life-changing prowess. I am honored to be sharing this journey called life with you. *Later in life, you are still kicking up dust and I love that about you. Hit the checkered flag with wheels smoking. You model what passion for life looks like.*

Lastly, Pastor Jentezen Franklin, our Senior Pastor, at Free Chapel in Gainesville, Ga (www.freechapel.org). I am humbled and blessed to be a member of Free Chapel. Your heart for God and your burden for souls are so evident each week. Thank you for still believing in the Old Rugged Cross and the power of the Word of God. In addition, you still believe in talking in tongues and the authority of the Holy Spirit. You don't cave into being Politically Correct or bend with the Societal Norms. As a man of unfathomable faith and sincerity, you are leading many to walk in similar paths. Blessings to you, Cherise, and your family as you fulfill God's directives for Free Chapel, global. Lorraine and I are so thankful to call you our Pastor.

Contents

Note: At the end of each chapter, there is a reflection time and several action items to complete. Please feel free to cut along the dotted line to carry them with you. This is meant to keep these steps in front of you at all times.

As a consideration: This book is designed to be used individually or as a small group study. The questions at the end can be asked in a round-table setting.

It's Your Move!

Every One - A Player

Generations come and generations go. Pages of calendars flip with unrelenting fashion. Nothing holds back the movement of time and society for that matter. In my years of high school, back in the early eighties, I remember a singer coming out with a song called "1999". If you are unfamiliar with this lyric, it basically says "We're going to party like it's 1999!" The close of a millennium deserves a throw-down. An all-out thrashing. A non-stop host of boogie banquets! At least, that is what the song promoted. But, for me, the thought that nearly 20 years would pass thus reaching toward 1999 was almost comical. "That seems so far away" many touted, including myself. Yet, one thing is for sure: those years did pass! Generations pass as well. Time marches on. Let's see this in print as anthropology shouts:

1. Silent Generation - Born 1945 or before
2. Baby Boomers - Born 1946 to 1964
3. Generation X - Born 1965 to 1976
4. Millennials or Gen Y - Born 1977 to 1995
5. Gen Z, IGen, or Centennials - Born 1996 to TBD

Do we have anything in common as generations? Is there a thread of oneness in our grand pursuit called Life? Do we all meet at a familiar junction point, no matter the age or generation? Millennials would wonder if the Silent Generation could ever relate to them. What about the Gen Z, IGen, or Centennials? Would they understand a Baby Boomer's view on life? In every assortment of life's outpouring, generations can collide with each other. And, they have. This fact fosters division. Is there a universal meeting spot? *I think there is.*

This book points to such a place. A recognizable summit or reference is found: *Expectations vs. Reality.* Can we all agree, no matter the generation, from the Silent Generation to the Centennials, that what we thought life would look like and what it turns out like is immensely different. *Can I get an Amen!*

In each life span, *everyone is a player in this game called Life.* You don't get to sit this one on the bench. You can't ask for a "pass" because you are in the information age or too "old" for that matter. Modern conveniences don't omit you from this reality, neither does retirement. Life will call you out, at every stage, from those born in 1945 to those recently born in 2019.

As you will discover throughout this book, I share stories while at ages: 13, 21, 27, 32, 38, 44, and today at 55. *How old are you right now?* While reading this, I think you will relate to each part. *How do I know?* That is easy. *Life can hurt. It usually does.* Everybody comes to this realization sooner or later. *Make it sooner.* And, what you do about it will determine if your life is a *Masterpiece on a Mission* or a *Menace of unfolding Misery.* Yes, Gen Xer, Baby Boomer, Millennialist, Centennials, and even you Silent Generation participants, we've ALL got work to do. Let's rise above the "REAL" we have and pursue the "IDEAL" we want. Let's grow in the process of processing Life's outcomes. Are you with me? We can do it together!

Gut-Level Honesty

In August 2010, I enrolled at Liberty University to earn a Master of Arts in Executive Leadership (I had planned to take my free electives in marriage counseling, though). It was also during this season that Lorraine and I were planning our upcoming wedding. Needless to say, it was a busy time for me. I began my classes with all the excitement of a child on Christmas morning. Yet, I had no idea the demands that graduate school would place on a person. There were lots of reading assignments, research papers, and writing projects. I waded through the majority of my tasks, but writing seemed to be effortless for me. I never got to tap into this side of my brain as a young mechanical engineering student. Nonetheless, while writing, I enjoyed being imaginative, insightful, and inspirational. To my surprise, each professor began to say the same thing, "You were born with an incredible gift to write and God is going to use you with this talent." I was blown away to say the least! One professor even compared me to the accomplished Author, Max Lucado, whose books occupy my shelves today. I was humbled and appreciative for his kind words. It only served to confirm what was in my heart from God. I have wanted to write books for a number of years and sense now is the time for my first one.

This book focuses on the *Life theme* of *Expectations vs. Reality* (See Pages xxi - xxii). As my life has unfolded over the past 30 years, I have gone from being the *eternal optimist* to being a *reformed optimist.* Please allow me to explain. When I was younger, including my teenage years, I believed that life was an unbelievable gift from God and that everything just worked out as you expected it would. Marriages lasted. Careers flourished. Physical health was sustained. Small businesses thrived. Real estate property appreciated. Mental health was possible. Resources were plentiful. Friendships benefited. The list goes on and on. Now, I know what you might be thinking, *"Only at Disney World does life work out like that."* That may be true. Still, I just believed the best about life (and people, too)! On the other hand, today, I must honestly admit that the gap between my *Expectations* of life and my *Reality* are looking a bit more like the Grand Canyon. If you are normal (whatever that means to you), I suspect your life plays out in a similar fashion. What's a person to do?

Enter this book, *"My Life is: Real vs. Ideal".* You are <u>not</u> alone if you have ever thought that life was not delivering what you had *expected* or *hoped* it would. In fact, you may be saying to yourself, *"Life really hurts!"* and many would agree with you. When I was in college, many eons ago, I saw a bumper sticker that said, "Life Stings…and Then You Die!" While this in-your-face appeal caught me quite off guard, it was stating the obvious, *"Life does not deliver!"* Can you relate to that? I think we *all* can!

I'm glad you have taken the time to read this book. I will go on record to acknowledge that life does hurt, sometimes. But, it still delivers! *Every experience, season, circumstance, and challenge seek to propel you forward and enhance your daily walk.* As we journey together, we can narrow your gap between Expectations and Reality.

Humbled and Blessed,

Marvin Robert (also known as "Bud")

Marvin Robert Wohlhueter, MA, Th.D., CLC

Here We Go!

In January of 1996, I was experiencing the best time of my life. I was in the early years of marriage as a young man and enjoying all the newfangled changes taking place (well, most of them). My wife (then) was pregnant with our first child, Raleigh Faith, and the thought of starting a new family was thrilling and scary all at the same time. Additionally, I was enrolled in Andersonville Theological Seminary's online program. I was preparing for pastoral ministry and transitioning out of my engineering career. I guess you could say I was on top of the world (or so I thought). In this season of my life's journey (February, 1996), I was approached by a pastoral search committee, several states away, who had gotten a pastoral resume of mine and invited my wife and me for a visit to their church to preach a trial message. This would have been a dream come true for me! To make a long story short, I was asked to be their new pastor after preaching that Sunday. While taking some time to pray and seek God, enthusiastically I accepted the position. I immediately started to preach and teach on the weekends there and we would wait to move until September when my daughter was born. Being several states away, it took some time to plan for our upcoming move. As the weeks neared, I found myself getting mentally ready to shepherd this small country church near Greensboro, NC (not the real location). Finally, we made the four-hour move and set up the parsonage (pastor's home) to prepare for our ministry there. The church was gracious enough to allow us to get the parsonage ready beforehand. During this period of time, I wanted to know what people really struggled with in life and how, as a young, budding pastor, God might help them to overcome these issues. I began to ponder what that list might consist of. *It captivated me!*

As the first several months passed, I began to see lives changing. People were genuinely thankful about what the Lord was doing there in Greensboro, NC. I was honored and indebted to God for His provision. On the other hand, behind the scenes of this small country church, the longstanding leadership team did not welcome my far-reaching approach to effective, life-changing ministry. I was visiting people far from God and inviting them to the church.

The church did a monthly homeless shelter ministry which was right across the street from the local "crack" house. On one particular Saturday night, we were locked in after hours. We fed the homeless people meals, washed their clothes, and encouraged them to pursue God's direction for their lives. After serving the evening meal, I went out to talk to the people as individuals. I went from cot to cot showing them the love of God. One gentleman said, "In all my times of coming here, you are the *first* person to ever come out and talk to us and treat us like human beings." I was gladdened and yet surprised. The next morning, I invited the whole group to come to church and I took our church van to pick them up. I could sense God was stirring in these people's lives.

This action, on my part, did not sit well with the vintage church leadership. I was crushed by their behavior. It was shocking to me! As tragic as it was, I was terminated as their Pastor late one August evening. It was just two weeks after my daughter was born. I, now, found myself with a new born baby, a post-partum wife, no source of income, no place to live, and four-hours from anything familiar. *My heart was absolutely devasted.* I experienced first-hand one of my new findings, *Expectations vs. Reality.* Could it be that what we expect life to look like and what it really turns out like is *vastly* different? I would be the first to proclaim a hearty *Amen* to that! During the next several months, while trying to pick up the pieces of my shattered heart, I composed the rest of my list of the Key Real-Life issues noted below as God spoke into my situation and life-dynamic. Over time, my heart began to heal and my days were slowly getting better. However, I could not shake this list of *Real-Life issues* or *Life Themes* (I like to refer to them as *Bombs*) that we all *must* face. Please read the list below and place a mental check mark besides the ones that jump out at you. I would guess that several strike a chord in your heart, mind, emotions, and have caused great distress in your life.

Key Real-Life Issues

Relationships ... Love

- <u>Family</u> - Relationships (Marriage / Remarriage / Blended Families)
- <u>Friendships</u> – Community – (Doing Life together – Being Accepted, Affirmed, and Appreciated)
- <u>Forgiveness</u> - Personal Peace / Relational Health (Living from an Inner Core of Peace)

Debt Elimination ... Security

- <u>Finances</u> - Home / Work (Earning, Budgeting, Tithing, Retirement, Generosity)

Career Development ... Fulfillment

- <u>Futures</u> - Goals / Purposes (Future-casting, Career Development, what is my Life's Purpose)
- <u>Failures</u> - Performance (Playing to win, rather than not to lose – Risk and Reward Dynamics)

<u>Personal Growth</u> ... Preparation

- <u>Fears</u> - Security (Known, Unknown, Internal, External, Self-talk Dynamics)
- <u>Faults</u> - Character (Weaknesses, habits, negative thinking, generational sins)
- <u>Fatigue</u> - Stress / Setting Priorities (Overloaded, Overcommitted, Living with NO personal margin)
- <u>Frustrations</u> - Expectations vs. Reality (the Gap between Your Real vs. Your Ideal)
- <u>Falsehoods</u> - Truths / Beliefs (Core beliefs from Childhood / Life's Experiences)
- <u>Feelings</u> - Emotions – (Inner Man: Interpretation, Perception, and Action)
- <u>Fitness</u> - Preventive Health (Rest, Diet, Exercise, Check-ups, Preventive Health)
- <u>Faith</u> - Spiritual Things (the Umbrella Topic: Is God Real, Relevant, Relational, Right, and My Response)
- <u>Favor</u> – The Edge You Need to Succeed - (Favor comes from Service to Others & Service to God)
- <u>Final Things</u> – Confronting Eternity, Embracing the After-Life

As the list depicts, there are four main headings under which the other subsets fall. These are as follows: *Relationships, Debt Elimination, Career Development, and Personal Growth.* Each play vibrant roles in your life. In fact, they tap into your basic human needs. Every human being wants to feel loved, secure, fulfilled, and prepared for real life. That is precisely why each category is so *strategic* in your life and important to God. It is equally true that Satan, your *real* enemy, would work so hard to make each category stressful, unproductive, and confusing. Still, if we lack growth in any one sub-topic, we feel vulnerable and ill-equipped to face life's ups and downs. This was *now* true in my own world under the sub-topic of *Expectations vs. Reality.*

Over the years, I have learned a great deal about this topic (willingly and not so willingly I might add). Please allow me to encourage, equip, and empower you in this crucial area. I will adopt a Life Coaching posture to unpack this material. Concurrently, as my worldview, I hold to a Christ-Centered stance. *There is no hidden agenda as a Follower of Christ on my part as Author; rather I am using this as my plumb line for Absolute Truth.*

One last thought in this chapter. You may have wondered why do I call these Life Themes: *Bombs?* I'm glad you asked. Each area listed above has the ability to blow up your life if you don't allow God to give you the insight, wisdom, and instruction to master each one. They will cause your life to become a chore and an energy draining existence. Nevertheless, your life can be different. Let's get started with the next chapter.

It's Your Move!

1. From the list, which of the four main categories brings the most trouble in your life: Relationships, Debt Elimination, Career Development, or Personal Growth? Why? What do you want to change about this main topic in the next 30 days, 3 months, 6 months and I year?

    a. 30 days: _____

    b. 60 days: _____

    c. 3 months: _____

    d. 6 months: _____

    e. I2 months: _____

2. Under your main category, what are the top two sub-categories. Why? How do you want to change them?

    a. 30 days: _____

    b. 60 days: _____

    c. 3 months: _____

    d. 6 months: _____

    e. I2 months: _____

1

A Unicorn, Mermaid, & Flying Elephant

Now that I have your attention, let's talk! What do unicorns, mermaids, and flying elephants *all* have in common? Come on. I know you can do it! Think hard. Time is about up. What is your answer? There may be several things in common, but the one that stands out most to me is that *they do not exist in Real life*. Nonetheless, from childhood, we have all read such stories, seen many delightful movies, pondered the worlds of the enchanted, day dreamed about Cinderella's glass slipper; role played to the likes of Peter Pan and Never Land, and wished we could be Super Heroes like Superman or Bat Man. Our imaginary ability is an influential tool for vision, creativity, expression and our imminent future.

As we move from the influences of Disney and our cognitive thinking develops, we begin to have people ask us what we want to *be* when we grow up. Here again, our limitless minds stretch to such noble professions as Fire Fighter, Police Officer, Doctor, or an Engineer (for little boys) to Ballerina, Nurse, Teacher, or Opera Singer (for little girls). This whimsical season of development may even have us combine several jobs, believing life can have multiple careers *all-at-once*. As parents, we even encourage such expressions of thought and affirm the belief that our children are destined for greatness by the hand of Almighty God. *And we should!* Destiny and nobility lie within the cells of our children's DNA and society needs the contributions each one can bring to humanity. *However,* I sometimes wonder in our optimism and validation if we have helped to construct an *unrealistic* and *unhealthy* expectation of life. Are we setting up our children for disappointment and heartache later on in life? *That is simply a point to ponder! You must decide that for yourself.*

Herein lies the *big* dynamic I want to expound on in this book and offer healing, help, and hope for those who have been *beat up* by life. Everyone carries a mental picture of what life should look like when he or she gets older. It has been an emerging picture from early childhood and travels well into adulthood. Many things have contributed to the image you hold such as family members, friends, school, television, societal norms, experiences (negative and positive), and expectations of self. Every day, you add brush strokes to the canvas of your evolving life, endeavoring to create the most beautiful scenery of promise, purpose, and fulfillment. Convinced you've got the world by the tail, you march forward with the conviction that *"I simply can not fail"* while working to pursue my conceptual picture. Off you go…college degree, two-story house, white picket fence, wonderful marriage, a couple of kids, and a family pet to name of few of life's simple treasures. *Everyone sets out with great expectations in this majestic drama called Life.* I, too, must admit it was amazing to start this process. And, I was ready to begin my ride. *I suspect you were too!*

Wake-Up Call 101…Life was not working out like my cerebral picture. What is going on here? What was I doing wrong? I can't believe this is happening to me! I am not prepared to handle all of the *sundry* challenges, experiences, disappointments, or set backs. I was a winner (so I thought and my parents affirmed) and life was dealing me a losing hand. To be completely transparent, I was angry and irritated by my present circumstances. *I felt cheated and let down by life's outcome.* Can you connect with my feelings of loss and frustration? *Have you been there yourself?* Don't worry! You're not alone. Every one of us has hit a wall called *"Reality"* and it pains us to say the least.

Let's examine it in more detail in the next chapter. I have good news for you in the pages to follow! Every opportunity for bad can turn out for good in God's Economy as noted in the power scriptural reference of Genesis 50:20, "You intended to harm me, but God intended it for good to accomplish what is now being done, the saving of many lives." *God always has the last word over your life.* That is good news, my Dear Friend. However, Reality still hurts! Let's explore this *"Bomb"* together!

It's Your Move!

1. What was your "mental picture" like of your emerging adulthood? Was it realistic? Why or Why Not?

2. What did you "dream" of becoming as a young child? Did you feel supported? Encouraged? Validated?

3. Do you relate to the theme: Expectations vs. Reality? Do you feel cheated by life? Have you been "robbed" in some way that you have not gotten over? Why? _____

4. What do you want to overcome in life? Can you envision a better tomorrow? List 2 things you want to create. a._____ b. _____

5. Genesis 50:20 states that God can turn our troubles into triumphs. How do you believe He is able to do this for your life's story? _____. Read aloud Genesis 50:20 over and over again for 5 times. Then, commit it to memory. God has the LAST word over you.

2

The Rugged Terrain of Reality

What comes to mind when I mention the words, Rugged Terrain? For some, it conjures up images of rock-laden mountains or dangerous cliffs. Others may think of a hot desert backdrop or barren plains. In any event, it is hard terrain to navigate and extremely difficult to make any *significant* progress in, or through. Now, what comes to mind when I speak of the "Rugged Terrain of Reality"? Does the same hold true? Whether you like it or not, *Life is a terrain*. It has the same individualities of a rock-laden mountain. Metaphorically, it is hard ground and sometimes it is very difficult to make any *significant* progress in, or through. We can all agree that we have faced times when what we expected from life and what we actually received felt like hard ground.

Life is a Rugged Terrain because you live with a constant tension, at play, every day of your life. It is the tension between the *Life Theme or Bomb, Expectations vs. Reality*. Let me explain to you in a tangible way you can relate to. My grandparents, on both sides of my parents, celebrated well over 50 years of marriage. My parents celebrated 53 years of marriage at the time of my mother's passing. It was wonderful to have a familial legacy of marital strength and commitment to surround my life. When I got married, at the age of 27 (notice I didn't rush into it), I had an expectation that I would follow in this same tradition of marital triumph passed down to me. *Sad to say, my first marriage ended after 16 years of marriage.* For the first time, divorce was introduced into my family lineage and my children would have to navigate its upcoming impact. My new <u>reality</u> was immeasurably different than my initial expectation.

Please allow me to further illustrate this point. After making a move to live closer (Athens, GA) to my (then) spouse's family in my mid-thirties, I was faced with a period of two years of joblessness (this devastates a man's soul). I had always worked hard and celebrated years of employment success. However, after two years of searching and sending out hundreds of resumes in a 60-mile radius, I was still without employment (my son, Jake, was 2 years old so I was Mr. Mom). This ripped into my self-worth as a man and being the provider of my family. I finally landed a *drafting job*, earning less than half of what I was making as a mechanical engineer, at a local manufacturing plant in northeast, Georgia. *I drove through 6 different counties to get to this job.* I left home at 6:00 am in the morning and traveled some 55 miles *one way*. Each evening, I would arrive back home at 6:30 pm only to find my wife (then) burdened and fearful about my declining financial ability to provide for our family's needs. I worked this job faithfully for a total of two years. Consequently, the stress took a toll on my physical body and emotions as well as my marriage. It was during this season that I, once again, felt the sting of this *Bomb*, Expectations vs. Reality.

Finally, in my mid-forties, I got remarried to a wonderful woman from Trinidad named Lorraine, in 2010, as previously stated. While I had children from a previous marriage, Lorraine and I had high aspirations to have a child or two of our own. We pondered the thoughts of being parents together. We spent hours talking about what our children might look like. It was exciting to dream of a day when little steps would be sounding across our hardwood floors. Months came and went as we planned for a pregnancy which then turned into years.

We tried a couple of different options towards achieving pregnancy which left us emotionally bruised, disappointed, and rather discouraged. Yet, we didn't want to give up the hope of being parents. After a period of healing, we wanted to try again to become parents. I must confess I was somewhat hesitant to try again so soon, but wanted to support my wife's desire for motherhood. To our great surprise, we were grateful to God when we got the news that Lorraine had conceived and was now 8 weeks pregnant. *Lorraine and I were walking on air!* I remember sitting in church reflecting on the goodness of God during the Thanksgiving week in 2012. We had so much to be thankful for. God had really met us in a big way.

Our free time was spent looking at cribs, strollers, baby clothes, toys, and contemplating baby names. Early in the morning hours, on the eve before Thanksgiving, I was awoken by Lorraine who was in extreme pain. We rushed to the emergency room of our local hospital. It crushed us immeasurably when the medical tests confirmed our worst nightmare. Lorraine had a miscarriage. Our tears started to flow and we were broken inside. *Our expectations were dashed by life's reality.* We now again turned to God for healing and our future direction.

What about you? What experiences come to mind as you ponder, *Expectations vs. Reality?* Did you ever think you would be the victim of spousal abuse? What about sexual abuse? What about an unexpected divorce? Would you have ever dreamed homelessness would be a chapter in your life's story? What goes through your mind when you find out you are pregnant during your senior year of high school and the future you've planned begins to drastically change? Can you identify with the young man who drinks to be socially accepted only to find himself addicted years later and needing Alcoholics Anonymous to break such a destructive habit? Do you know the pain of finding letters in a shoebox that reveal a longstanding relationship of your mate with another lover? Have you first-hand experience with the doctor's pronouncement of cancer and the numbness you felt as you digested the news. Has corporate downsizing given you your walking papers months before your long-anticipated retirement?

These are just a few of the many tragedies we must face in this unpredictable journey called Life. *We've all been at the crossroads of Expectations and Reality.* Where do you go and what do you do when life's reality has robbed you of vitality, passion, imagination, and faith? Please allow me to escort you as you learn "Proven practices to creating a fulfilling life." *We can do it, together!*

It's Your Move!

1. Life is a Rugged Terrain. Do you agree or disagree with this statement? Why or why not? _____

2. We've all been at the crossroads of Expectations vs. Reality. What has that been like for you? _____. Can you zero in on a time when you were unsure what to do next? _____.

3. What can be learned when LIFE does not produce what we expected? Are you blaming others, yourself, God, etc? a. _____

   b. _____

4. They say "HOPE" is the rescuer of dreams when expectations and reality don't match up. On a scale of 0 (low) and 10 (high), how do you rate your "Hope" scale today? What would it take to improve it more by 1 point?

   0_____5_____10

3

No Stranger to Disappointment

I come to you today as a tour guide of life rather than a travel agent. Please let me explain the difference. As mentioned, my wife hails from the Island of Trinidad. When we first met, she would describe in detail the beauty and splendor of her homeland. She even went to the extent of sending me photo after photo of places she had been to and the brilliance of the Caribbean wonderland. She had sent me one postcard that just looked larger than life from Tobago (a sister island) and I made the comment, "Can this be real?" At the time, when others would ask me about Lorraine's country, I could only describe what she had conveyed to me in words and pictures. I did my best to adequately inform my listener of Trinidad's majesty. I was acting as a travel agent for this delightful country as I had never been there.

Then, December 2010 came. I made my first visit to this sought-after island paradise. I left on Christmas Eve at 6:30 in the morning. I had butterflies in my stomach, much like a person about to deliver his or her first speech. I could not wait to find out for myself the uniqueness of this island get-away. It took me all day to travel as flight after flight was delayed and shifted around on Christmas Eve. Growing weary from the travel demands, I wondered if it would be worth the wait. I finally touched ground in Trinidad at 11:30 pm (some 17 hours later). Exhausted, hungry, and a little disoriented, I made my way through customs and the baggage claim area. What I experienced once outside lifted all the day's travel demands. The island was alive during Christmas time and I saw evidence, right off the bat of an amazingly wonderful people. Being late into the night, I did not get to see any island beauty as of yet. However, the next morning, I made my way too many new locations that only confirmed what Lorraine had already experienced for herself.

On the third day of my trip, I was taken to the sister island called Tobago via ship (about 2 hours travel). I was exposed to the scenery like no other. I saw lush greenery, dazzling flowers everywhere, mountains proudly standing guard around these sister islands, and scores of views that would take your breath away. Once in Tobago, we ended up at one of the docks which featured a boating backdrop. My mind immediately recalled the photo once sent to me from my dear wife. Now, I was standing at the very location that produced such a captivating postcard. *It was real and I was there!* Now, I experienced it first hand. I was no longer describing a place I had never been. Now, I can now tell people I had been to Trinidad and Tobago and I crossed over the finish line from travel agent to tour guide. Now, I am sharing from what I know personally, rather than what I have been told. *This qualifies you in a different way, A totally unique way!*

Let's transfer this line of thinking to Life. I have walked the road of pain and suffering in my short pilgrimage on earth. I have been through so much that many would think I am making it all up. *I wish I could say I were!* No, every experience is real and has refined me into the person I am today. It has not been easy, *but I can relate to others in a way that most can not.* As they say, "Been there, done that, and have the

T-Shirt to prove it." I once had my Best Friend, John, tell me "Bud, you don't have to be the poster child for every type of dysfunction in life." *I must confess I have seen my share of challenges.*

Please allow me to illustrate my point with a shortened, laundry list of some of the things I have had to face since my sixteenth birthday until the present. This is by no means a plea for sympathy or pity. I have learned to be an overcomer by the grace of God. Has it been hard? Sure! Have I learned during each trial, you bet! It is my prayer that I can encourage you to press on in spite of your current circumstances.

Let me begin by sharing my health challenges. In the summer between my freshman and sophomore year, I was told I had to have both my ankles operated on as a result of a football injury. I agreed to give-up the summer to complete the necessary surgery. In addition, I had constant nasal and breathing issues through the years. So, the doctors all suggested taking care of everything at <u>one</u> time. What sounded good in theory did not make for an abundant summer. I had casts on both legs up to my knees and a nose packed full of gauze. I looked like I had been run over by a tractor trailer. It took <u>all</u> summer to recover from both surgeries. I had months of physical therapy as I learned to walk again. It was comforting to finally shed the granny walker and move about on my own two feet. As for my nose, it healed and I could breath freely and had good air flow. It was worth the effort on both counts. I learned a great deal about perseverance and determination, first hand, that summer. Ironically, I would have my nose operated on two more times in the next four years to correct continuing breathing issues. My friends often joked that I got cosmetic changes to my nose. I would say, "No silly, I just want to breath like normal people".

In the summer of 1985, I was given the awesome opportunity to work with IBM (Big Blue as they called it then) as an Intern in Atlanta, Georgia. When you are a broke college student, IBM sounded like an ideal way to make serious money, gain career experience, and maybe make some contacts for an upcoming future. I learned a lot that summer and met a Customer Service Manager who just moved from Boulder, Colorado to Atlanta. In our initial conversation of all of 15 minutes, I told him I would love to live in Colorado, one day, if anything ever came open. He assured me he would keep me in mind with his fellow contacts as he took my phone number and contact information. *It absolutely left my mind that day.*

Well, life marched on and I was attending Southern Tech (as we used to call Southern Polytechnic State University which is now Kennesaw State University) and was dreaming of Christmas vacation, my next big time off. As Christmas break finally arrived, I was looking forward to a little rest and relaxation. Late one evening, I was washing dishes after a family meal, just days before Christmas. The phone rang and my mom told me it was for me. I dried my hands and took the call. It was an IBM college-intern manager calling from Boulder, Colorado. They wanted me to do an internship with them, starting in early January.

Here was my dilemma. I had just interviewed earlier in the week for a co-op job at a defense contractor in northwest Atlanta and was awarded the position to start in early January, after the holidays. IBM, too, wanted me to decide about the position in a week and start in January. *To be honest, I was shocked that they even called me.* I really never imagined this would have materialized. I wrestled for days with this decision. My parents allowed me to make up my own mind. I was so torn because I had a good thing already. Did I want to risk this for an unknown position in Colorado? I distinctly remember the days of trial, trying to decide over my career tug-o-war. I spoke with the IBM manager often and he gave me the encouragement to simply give it a try. In the end, I took the IBM position. Who wouldn't want to live in Colorado?

I packed up my VW Scirocco and headed West. When I arrived in Boulder, I was a little scared to be so far from the familiar, but I was willing to make a go of it. Everything was going great, or so I thought. When I checked into what it would cost to attend the University of Colorado (Go Buffalos) in Boulder, I quickly realized I would be financially unable to attend classes as I would be paying my own way now as an out-of-state tuition student. When I called the IBM manager, they conveyed that they would not be able to offer any financial assistance because the internship did not allow for tuition help. I was distraught to say the least! *I was instantly gripped with fear.*

I had a big decision to make and I was not sure what to do. I felt like I had <u>failed</u> in my decision to take the IBM job (at least I initially thought that). I had never faced failure before with such magnitude. For the most part, I had been able to accomplish everything I ever attempted and now I was feeling the sting of defeat. In the end, I decided to return to Atlanta and pursue my education at the college I was already attending. I would just have to wait until the next quarter started. It really messed with my self-esteem and self-worth as a person, though. *I experienced some dark days as a result of this season.*

I had lost the defense contractor opportunity, college had already started and I found myself with nothing to do. My father was not going to let me sit around the house and nurse my wounded heart and emotions. No, I was told to find work and I began a retail job at K-Mart until I could start back to school the next quarter. *Humble Pie at its best!* I went from IBM or Lockheed-Martin to working in the automotive department at K-Mart, stocking oil, spark plugs and making spare keys for customers. *However, it started me on a spiritual search for answers which ultimately lead me into a personal relationship with Jesus Christ in March, 1986.* I completely surrendered my life to Christ and I have never been the same since. Good from Bad! That's the God I serve (Genesis 50:20, at its best).

Life marched on with college graduation, marriage at age 27, *and a calling on my life to minister to hurting people.* My eagerness to serve others was born right out of my own experience to have others know the hope and peace that I found in God. I attended seminary and earned both a Masters and Doctorate in Theology in 1995 and 2002, respectively. However, after two short-lived attempts of serving in pastoral ministry and learning how challenging church people can be, my wife (then) was reluctant to continue on this path and our marriage began to be impacted as a result of such excruciating experiences. I found myself back into the grind of mechanical engineering and working to provide for my wife and daughter, *but things were never the same.*

By the fall of 2006, I had entered into a state of clinical depression and anxiety. I was broken-hearted. I was not sleeping at night (for years). I couldn't concentrate. I was severely fatigued. I was lonely. I was suffering emotionally and mentally.

Sadly, my marriage ended and became final in May, 2008. I found myself starting over in life at age 43 with an 11-year-old daughter and a 7-year-old son. I was now a single parent, a place I never dreamed would be my reality. It was a perplexing time for me. *But, I serve a God with redemptive power and His healing waters of grace has brought me through!*

This is just a small snapshot in time of my Real-life experiences. I have walked a road few can relate to and I am determined to help others who have looked life in the face and declared, *"I will survive and thrive in spite of my obstacles".* You can join them in their sentiment. You can *overcome* as I have today by the hand of God! Let's explore deeper our Expectations of life and our unfolding Reality that makes it so hard to navigate. The theme of Real vs. Ideal will be explained in the next chapter.

It's Your Move!

I. In life, we have all experienced our share of disappointments. What would you say are your top 3 that you can remember?
    a._____ b._____ c. _____.

2. How did you conquer these times of stretching and trials? _____. Did you feel that God was "picking" on you? Why or Why not?

3. Have you become bitter at life's hardships? _____. Do you isolate yourself to prevent others from hurting you? _____. What would you tell someone in your "shoes"? _____. Are you willing to grow from this?

4. Do you have the spirit of a "Warrior"? "I will survive and thrive in spite of my obstacles!" Is this your battle cry? _____.

5. Has God been a part of your healing process? _____.

4

Your Real vs. Your Ideal

This chapter and insight can be extremely liberating for you. The balancing act between these two spectrums can be quite testy, but the payoff is incredible. Let's begin with the obvious. Life is filled with the REAL. 24/7 – 365 days a year, Life is raw! The every day details of marital strains, communication breakdowns, financial pressures, career demands, parenting pitfalls, soccer mom schedules, and changing personal dynamics can leave us feeling overwhelmed, fearful and sometimes helpless, or even hopeless. Today, as I sit in a coffee house in Greenville, South Carolina to write this chapter, the store is actively filling cup after cup of java, the stimulant of choice - even at 6:00 am. In the United States (my homeland), we thrive on building into our lives hustle and bustle, but we drink energy drinks to facilitate the pace of this demand. The energy drink industry is a billion-dollar-a-year industry. Why? We need these additives to give us the kick to get everything done today. We have all seen the various energy drinks at the grocery store and various convenience stores.

In fact, we live in a world that demands the envelope of success be pushed to the maximum. I would venture to say that we often feel guilty if we have any down-time in our day. Weekends were once a time for rest, relaxation, reflection, and restoration. However, today, they are filled with travel, sports teams, hobbies, shopping, trips, and church demands. We would feel unproductive to burn a Saturday doing little to nothing with our to-do list activities. That is just where we are as a Culture.

Consequently, the effects are noticeable. We roll into Monday morning exhausted and weary from the weekend. What is the outcome? *We feel overloaded physically, mentally, emotionally, spiritually, and relationally.* If we are completely honest with ourselves, we wish life were different and the enjoyment of life richer, purposeful, and refreshing. Together, we can begin to change the present to make way for a healthier future.

Contrasting the REAL, in walks Mr. and Mrs. IDEAL. They are sporting the perfect balance of marital satisfaction, communicative excellence, budgetary obedience, career fulfillment, parenting mastery, personal growth passion, and scheduling perfection. Mr. and Mrs. IDEAL are never out of sorts with time because they have arrived at the *textbook* mixture of life dynamics, charting a magnificent tapestry of relational health, debt elimination, career development, and personal growth.

I know what you're thinking," I'm about to be sick, but let me kick him or her in the knee, first!". Does Mr. and Mrs. IDEAL make you sick? *They make everyone sick if we were gut-level honest!* I can hear you saying to yourself, "No one can have that kind of life in today's fast-paced, get-it-done world." Is that thought echoed deep in your heart and soul? Your reservation with such a life is that it appears unrealistic and unattainable. Nonetheless, your attraction to such a life causes your mind to imagine how liberating this kind of blend could be. The internal tug-o-war of your REAL vs. your IDEAL rages every moment of your life's passing. I know its true because I look into the eyes of people today and I see their <u>frustration</u>. It is very evident and tangible! I would heartily agree that the tension is constant and relentless, but let's just say that it is the target to shoot for as you move from your REAL to your IDEAL. *On a side note, I am facing the same frustrations in my own world. We're ALL in the same boat!*

Now, let me give you a sentence to memorize that will bring you closer to the life you've dreamed of living. I believe this small understanding will begin to generate life and vitality into your ever-changing sphere. Here it is! First, break down the word, "ideal" into two components "I" and "deal". What you recognize right off the bat is the "I", a personal pronoun. This conjures up the belief that it is personal and possible. "I" puts you in the driver's seat and empowers you to think about life in a different way than it exists today. It is liberating because it cuts away all the neighboring weights that you might feel are holding you back. Change is possible and probable because of "I". Next, check out the second part of the word, "deal", a verb. To "deal" represents action, intent, and initiative. *It puts Motion to Notion.* Did you catch that last phrase? Let me repeat it for emphasis. *It puts <u>Motion</u> to <u>Notion</u>!* Dealing is the key. However, also know that "deal" can be a noun as well.

Let me explain it this way. Many years ago, in the 1970's, there was a successful TV show called "Let's Make a Deal". You may or may not be familiar with the show, but let me give you the punch line. Every contestant was given the option to *trade up* to something better than they currently had with him or her. For example, a contestant may have a deck of cards that the announcer would offer him or her $50 dollars for. The aspiring contestant would happily agree and now have a quick $50. However, the announcer would then offer a chance to trade up to a better outcome, a new kitchen, an exotic trip, or sports car. The announcer would say something like, "You can keep your $50 dollars or trade it for what's behind Door # 1, Door

2, or Door # 3. Hence, the game title, "Let's Make a Deal". It made for great entertainment because it was NOT always a trade up as many contestants found out. I watched contestant after contestant get a donkey, a wash tub, a junk car, or some other second-hand prize. Therefore, it was imperative for the contestant to choose wisely for the deal swap. You must do the same in life!

Therefore, as I (pronoun) - Deal (verb) for a better deal (noun) in life, I can make my real world move in the direction of my ideal world. Here how it looks:

$$As\ I => Deal => REAL => IDEAL$$

Please internalize the progression of this formula. You <u>must</u> embrace this truth for a fruitful future! Notice the ownership here. Ponder the present tense dynamics. Catch the hope for a healthier tomorrow. *By now, you should be shouting as you read this!* You are <u>not</u> a prisoner of your REAL. You may have been Missing in Action (MIA) for years because you have been led to believe your life can never hold the promise you thought it should, or be any different than today. That is a lie from the devil, himself. You can change your world moving forward! You can take off the shackles of realism and move along the whimsical roadway to newness and passion. But, you have to be willing to deal.

A first cousin to the concept of REAL and IDEAL that we need to add to our discussion are the words, *contentment* vs. *complacency*. These two words, likewise, create a tension that you must monitor and master. Because they are always varying, you can get irritated with them. Why? Here is the rub as I see it. At any given moment in life, you have to be guarded and wise because you need to have contentment, but you should never get complacent, either, about your life. This tight-rope walk is challenging since it involves the heart, mind, and emotions.

If I were to ask if you are a contented person, what would you say? Now, be honest! What would others say? How about your spouse? Or your children? Your parents? Your best friend? It is very important to wrestle this down because the quality of your life hinges on what I am about to share with you. *Are you content with your present situation?*

Now, here is the other side of the coin to consider. If I were to ask if you are a complacent person, what would you say? Are you complacent with your present situation? Complacency can be toxic to the beauty of life. Human nature moves in the direction of this negative outcome. Our society is laden with the belief that I would rather do less and have less. Many have come to grips with a lackluster life and are perfectly fine with less than God created them for. How tragic a prognosis. Life is a gift to be unwrapped, daily. Never surrender to the enemy of complacency. Never! Never! Never!

Please allow me to break it down in its simplest form. I think this should help you. Every day, as I look at my REAL, I cannot be complacent about my current lack of progress <u>and</u> I must be content and grateful to God for the progress I have made moving toward my IDEAL. I realize that might sound confusing and problematic. It really is easier than you think in the long run. The key understanding is that life is fluid and not stationary. Never ever settle for less than God intended your life to become! When movements toward change seems slow, it is easy to grow weary and land on the bullseye of complacency. Here, you say things like, "What's the use? This is just the way it is and I have to accept that and move on." I totally understand as I have been there too often, myself. But, let me encourage you to press on in spite of what appears to be a lack of progress. God is not interested in your *pace* as much as He is your *progress*. The movements you've made toward change must be celebrated! *Do you celebrate the movements you've made?*

Here is where the word contentment must be considered. Being <u>thankful</u> is key in the wake of continual change. You must give thanks at <u>all</u> times, even in the momentary set-backs. The best is still yet to come. I really believe that about your life and future dynamics.

It can be remarkable. As the old saying goes, "I am not where I want to be, but I am not where I used to be, either." I want to give you a high-five if you can accept that statement. *Growth must be an awareness of both contentment and complacency.*

I hope you don't mind me throwing in a few Bible verses that help to illustrate this point for you. Don't worry! These verses are helpful and have no hidden agenda.

⁶ Yet true godliness with contentment is itself great wealth. ⁷ After all, we brought nothing with us when we came into the world, and we can't take anything with us when we leave it. ⁸ So if we have enough food and clothing, let us be content. *Godliness with contentment is great gain.* I Timothy 6:6-8 (NLT) – Italics added.

In this dialogue with the young, upcoming preacher, the Apostle Paul, his mentor, is helping Timothy see the *big* picture about life and the difference between contentment and complacency. He is encouraging the young lad not to get hung up with the stuff of life, but rather grow what truly matters in the end of life, the eternal things. Why? Paul sets the record straight when he tells the rising student that life does not make its boast in possessions, power, prestige, or position. In fact, he dials it down to the basics. Food, clothing, faith, and purpose should be the elements of contentment. You will exit this life with nothing! We all know this truth as we have buried loved-ones with no U-haul behind the casket.

The Apostle Paul, in another passage, warns his readers of the hazards of complacency, too. ¹² I do not mean that I am already as God wants me to be. I have not yet reached that goal, but I continue trying to reach it and to make it mine. Christ wants me to do that, which is the reason he made me his. ¹³ Brothers and sisters, I know that I have not yet reached that goal, but there is one thing I always do. *Forgetting the past and straining toward what is ahead,* ¹⁴ I keep trying to reach the goal and get the prize for which God called me through

Christ to the life above. Philippians 3:12-14 (NCV). I italicized the key principle.

Let's take a look at one final aspect of REAL vs. IDEAL. It fleshes itself out in the awareness of Risk vs. Reward. If I could give you a word picture to grab hold of, it would be the following illustration. In your pocket, on any given day, I would instruct you to carry around three coins. These three coins would serve to facilitate the ingredients of this chapter. The first coin would flag the concept of REAL vs. IDEAL. The second coin would birth the tenets of Contentment vs. Complacency. The final coin would drive home the concept of Risk vs. Reward. These three coins signify the duality of life as you know it today. Truthfully, there is always a heads and tails in everyday living. A 50/50 chance of getting it right is the best you can strive for. However, just keep flipping your coins! Don't grow exhausted while doing so. NFL teams who lose the coin toss in the first half of the game receive the ball at the start of the second half. They get a chance to make up some ground. So, do you! Flipping coins is part of life. A good part!

So, what is the big idea of Risk and Reward...the heads and tails of your daily life today. Just the thought of it makes my heart race with passion, conviction, and intrigue. We see it all around us and we accept its premise. Big Risk...Big Reward. Small Risk...Small Reward. No Risk...No Reward. I like to think that life gives you options and the power of choice. Sure, you can calculate some of the risks and seek to minimize the effects of exposure to loss. However, in the grand scheme of things, there must be an acceptance of this coin in your proverbial pocket. Risk and Reward are part of the DNA of life.

Everyone must live with this tension as well, Risk vs. Reward. Please allow me to clarify this point in this manner. When I landed the job previously mentioned, driving some 55-miles each way to work, I was genuinely thankful for the job, but knew that I was capable of so much more. My engineering degree prepared me to do design, calculations, and analysis. Here, at this job, I was simply creating detail drawings for kitchen and bathroom renovations and new construction. Needed? Most definitely. However, far less than my giftedness and education. I likened it to a medical doctor taking blood pressure readings for his patients. Sure, it was pertinent information, but he was trained for so many grander things!

In the two years that I worked at this manufacturing plant, I shared life with three unique gentlemen (there names are not listed or location named). Each will shed insight into the Risk vs. Reward coin. Employee # 1 had been at the plant for a while. He was well educated from a good school in Pennsylvania and was serving in a prominent position. He often stated he wanted to work elsewhere, but was too <u>comfortable</u> in his lifestyle and did not want to upset the apple cart. This puzzled me greatly. He spelled it our for me one day and then I finally connected the dots. He stated, "I am happy with my nice house, lake toys, big truck and country living. I don't want to jeopardize <u>this</u> lifestyle I have built for myself. It's not worth it." Ouch! Risk vs. Reward tug-o-war at its best. Employee # 1 did not want to Risk anything for a different future.

Then there was Employee # 2. He had been at the plant for many years. He was a faithful employee and did his time each day. There was a longing in his heart to pursue other interests, but he was too old to begin such an uncertain journey. Not today! Can you believe it? Too old? What does that mean, anyway? Once again, Risk vs. Reward were slugging it out in the ring of life. This time, complacency was providing some Gatorade for the boxing match. Employee # 2 settled for the familiar and was dying a slow death inside each day.

Lastly, there was Employee # 3, He was a hard worker. Kind-hearted, spirited, energetic, able, and attentive to details. He worked countless, long hours to help grow the business. He almost seemed to sleep at the plant. Adding new machinery, increasing order demands, expanding inventory, and capital investments kept him hopping. Sadly though, I learned he had a new bride, a young son, and a newborn on the way. I wondered if his family got what they needed from him. Here, his Risk vs. Reward took on a different spin: *personal ownership of one's life vs. expectations of his employer.* He stated that Risk and Reward dynamics were not his to choose. Employee # 3 conceded to the pressure of expectations. *He simply sold his options.!*

One day, Employee # 1 turned the question back on me. He boldly said, "Why are you working at this factory if you have so many big dreams in your heart?" He wanted to know my story and why I was wasting my time at a do-nothing job, in going-nowhere, Georgia. I shared the dreams and aspirations of my heart to help hurting people and equipping them to succeed at life. This day I showed him that lowly places make the Rewards even sweeter if you continually are willing to trade up with each Risk. I used to tell him that my 55-mile ride each day was like heading to the backside of the desert as Moses did for his father-in-law, Jethro and the family business. *Obscurity is never tranquil living and nevertheless is often part of God's masterful plan for each life.* This was certainly true for mine. I would often weep as I drove to this job because I didn't understand the dynamics at play here. *But, God knew! He always does.*

I feel it is beneficial to hit the pause button for a minute and let me tell you what I am *NOT* suggesting for my factory co-workers. Employee # 1, "Just quit your job." Employee # 2, "Take a leap of faith at any age." And, Employee # 3, "Tell your employer that you want to do your own thing." By all means...No, No, No. I am not saying that! Nonetheless, what I am suggesting is *dream* of a better tomorrow. Consider your options. Unleash your inner destiny. Give energy to what it might embrace. You have to push against living every moment in a rut or feeling stuck. God has so much more for you than that. As you consider these three coins in your legacy pocket, give change a try. Know that it will feel a little awkward at first, but moving in that direction is healthy. Anytime you give up something old to gain something new, there is a feeling of loss, like part of you is dying. Loss brings grief and sadness. You feel displaced for a while. That is OK and normal! You will never regret trading up to an IDEAL way of living, but there is risk with every step you take. Press on anyway! The reward is so worth it.

Let's go back to my factory experience. This job taught me many lessons over the two years of tenure. As mentioned, I had a lot of time to think while I was driving. I had many conversations with God and often dialogued about my future. I had ample time to ponder the nuggets of gold that emerged from the six words in this chapter. REAL vs. IDEAL, Contentment vs. Complacency, and Risk vs. Reward. I will never be the same today because of my tenacious spirit for more in life. I am wanting God's best for my own life, every day, and its unfolding purpose. *I want the same for you!* Open up your being to alterations! Embrace it. Give into it. Stretch for it. Enjoy it. And, then, *Rejoice over it!* The world is watching!

As we move into the next chapter, I want to prepare you for the road ahead. It is an eye-opener for sure. Life is filled with challenges, hurdles, obstacles and pitfalls. It is so hard at times! Why? Good question. Let's explore it in Chapter 5.

It's Your Move!

1. Real vs. Ideal. Can you relate to these two words? Where does life find you more? _____.

2. Contentment vs. Complacency. Do you struggle to find balance between the two? How? _____.

3. Risk vs. Reward. Where do you concentrate your focus? Are you a risk-taker? Do you live in your comfort zone? What is stopping you from stepping out? _____.

4. I spent two years doing something "less than I was trained for" with my family's good in mind. Would you be willing to do so? _____. Why or Why not? _____.

5. List two things God is teaching you during this season of your life with these concepts:

    a. _____.

    b. _____.

5

Why Is Life So Hard?

Have you ever stopped dead in your tracks when an unexpected event came your way? Have you felt unprepared for a recent outcome? Have you laid awake, in the early hours of the morning, contemplating your next move in a familial dispute? Have you been the gossip train victim of a home foreclosure and imminent bankruptcy? What about the latest contestant in a down-sizing merger? Who knew you would be the person to wear the bad report about your child's silent, drug addiction? Do you keep a *For Sale* sign in the garage just in case you have to move quickly to protect your reputation? (maybe that's just me...I'm kidding!). Where and when will it all end? The list can be an exhausting. We've all faced things that were just plain H.A.R.D. Can we all agree on that? Life is extremely hard and even brutal, at times! Let's just throw that out on the table to gander at. 24/7 x 365 days hard! Why? Let me try to shed some light on that question in this Chapter. As you might expect, *we need to eat this elephant one bite at a time.*

Let's begin with some basic understandings before I dig into this topic further. There is no way in the scope of this chapter, or this book for that matter, to determine the difficulties of every life on planet Earth. I know that millions of people are walking through things that are unimaginable to the human mind and spirit. My heart breaks for your current circumstances and present suffering. Additionally, I am fully aware that mental health is <u>never</u> to be taken lightly or for granted. I have marched the road of anxiety and depression myself and know the anguish and pain it can cause as well as the years lost in its wake. Finally, I am not trying to give you a condensed version of a developmental psychology class which deals with the stages of life, personal growth dynamics, and cognitive advancement. Yes, I have studied developmental psychology and it is intense with a whole lot to learn. Thankfully, I did well in the class and garnered a wealth of knowledge. I'll apply <u>only</u> what is relevant in this chapter.

With that being said, this chapter deals more with my 25-plus years of interaction and involvement with people on a personal level. From my pastoral life, to corporate life, to little league ball games, to PTA meetings, to small group studies, and Chuck-e-Cheese visits, I have made myself a student of people in a very real way. I was willing to get messy as they shared <u>REAL</u> life stories with me. I was available to wade through the muck of life's complications with individuals and cared enough to lend a heart and a hand. I am no Mother Teresa, by no means. However, I was determined to understand people at a deeper level and comprehend what makes them navigate life as they do. Every conversation, every observation, every question asked, every tear shed, every embrace provided, all helped me to come up with my *Key Life Issues* as noted in the Introduction. I am forever grateful for their honesty, transparency, and vulnerability.

There were 16 main issues that I discovered as noted earlier that fall under 4 main headings: *relationships, debt elimination, career development,*

Marvin Robert Wohlhueter, Th.D.

and *personal growth*. Why, you ask, are these 4 main headings so pivotal and powerful in one's life? Why do they collide and cause confusion in our every day walk? I believe these two questions can be summed up this way. As God's creation, we all have basic human needs. These needs are played out in the following manner as noted earlier in this book. Let me share the four again for emphasis. Listed below are the Key Areas, in no order of importance:

- Relationships - *Love*
- Debt Elimination - *Security*
- Career Development - *Fulfillment*
- Personal Growth - *Preparation*

Relationships - Number #1. There is a need to feel loved, relationally. This need is hard-wired into your psyche and it cannot be overlooked. Everyone must feel the warmth of affection, approval, affirmation, and acceptance from others in his or her life. It is basic to your existence on planet Earth. It is at the core of your DNA. As much as individuals would claim, "I can make it *all* on my own", the truth is you can't. God created you as a *relational being.* Your life was meant to be a series of meaningful and sustainable relationships to bring you joy, interaction, and completeness. You <u>need</u> relationships and relationships need you. It is a partnership that will carry you into eternity. In fact, the Bible points to this fact from the very beginning when God placed Adam in the Garden of Eden and asked him to provide oversight for it. Then, God created Eve and produced the first marital couple. Together, they were to manage what God had created and enjoy the benefits of their relational interaction under the canopy of God's direction. However, with the introduction of rebellion and disobedience to God's commands, sin entered the world and caused a *cosmic meltdown. Now,* relationships are challenging and troublesome. *Now,* relationships have self-seeking motives and agendas. *Now,* relationships can be broken and lives can be destroyed in the fallout. Yes, your life becomes hard because relationships are *hard*.

Finances - Number #2. There is a need to feel secure, financially. Money, debt, credit cards, over-spending, mortgage payments, groceries, braces, and budgets. Hence, *anything* related to money in your life brings stress, worry, and confusion. We've all been there when an unexpected car repair shows up or when the washing machine dies. Yes, we see the money come in and we see the money go out. It is like a revolving door that we walk through each month. Only, it does not feel like a pastime we can win and often causes us to feel <u>unsecure</u> monetarily. I don't know about you, but money matters can be *huge* in every home life. The key word that comes to mind when money is discussed is <u>*pressure*</u>. Money, or lack of money, can create extreme pressure in our lives. This pressure can cause us to react in all kinds of ways, some of which may be unhealthy and unproductive. It happens every day in homes across America and around the world. Economic times, recessions, corporate-downsizing, and real estate blues can cause financial hardships. Let's dial it in distinctively for sake of learning. When the recession of 2008 hit America, many found themselves upside-down on their mortgages. For the first time in our life span, people actually owed *more* on their homes than they were worth. In my era of living, real estate was always a safe investment strategy. You could expect to appreciate annually 5 – 7% on your home and <u>always</u> sell it for a profit whenever you were ready to make a move. In this time window, however, that was not the case. In many communities in the United States (specifically Atlanta where I live today), the ability to sell your home had been eliminated because of today's economic strain. This restriction found countless families in dire straits because of their financial limitations. (As a side note, in 2017 - 2019, there has been some day light on the real estate burdens of the past decade) The end result of one's financial challenges makes life *hard*.

Career Development — Number #3. There is a need to feel fulfilled, vocationally. Statistics show that 7 out of every 10 individuals will wake up every morning, shower, get some breakfast and morning coffee, and make the daily commute to a job he or she hates. Yes, I said *hates!* What? How is that possible? Maybe, hate is too strong of a word! How about *extreme purposelessness?* A job without a purpose will never bring fulfillment, no matter how hard you try or how long you stay engaged mentally or employed physically. The key word for vocational interests is *fulfillment.* In your human need's bank, you have to make daily deposits of fulfillment or the years of working will leave you as a shell of a human being. *Fulfillment is at the core of who you are as an individual, vocationally.*

Let's dig a little deeper for understanding. Every job activity must find its way moving toward fulfillment, at some level, to bring meaning, value and, dedication. There was a study done in which individuals were paid $20 dollars to move a mound of dirt from one location to another. A long list of college students was chosen and a team assembled. With fire and tenacity, the team moved the dirt pile as requested and made their money in record time. The test was conducted the next day and this test was repeated for seven days. Much to the amazement of the testers, the number of college students interested began to drop during the seven days, even though $20 dollars was a great wage for the task (and for college students). Over time, the number of interested participants plunged to nearly nothing and ultimately to zero. Why? There appeared to be no purpose in just moving dirt from one location to another, even though the earnings were higher than working at a restaurant, office supply store, or retail chain as college students would. This test proved our basic human need for Career Fulfillment. At the end of the every day, individuals need fulfillment to survive and thrive in their career aspiration. Hence, life is *hard* because of Career dynamics.

Personal Growth — Number #4. There is a REAL need to feel prepared for life, personally. Personal Growth is <u>not</u> optional for individuals who want to become better husbands, wives, sons, daughters, co-workers, friends, neighbors, church members, and citizens. The reality is no one stumbles into the preparation needed to navigate life's changing aspects successfully. On-lookers often marvel at those who weather storms and difficulties as if they have been given a dose of doggedness from an outside source. Sure, they may have an active faith in God and that is necessary. However, the lion's share of people who overcome life's challenges have done so because they were prepared before they were hit. The Bible speaks of this situation as found in Matthew 7:24-27 (CEB)

[24] "Everybody who hears these words of mine and puts them into practice is like a wise builder who built a house on bedrock. [25] The rain fell, the floods came, and the wind blew and beat against that house. It didn't fall because it was firmly set on bedrock. [26] But everybody who hears these words of mine and doesn't put them into practice will be like a fool who built a house on sand. [27] The rain fell, the floods came, and the wind blew and beat against that house. It fell and was completely destroyed."

Here, Jesus is speaking specifically about preparation for the storms of life. Your foundation and its ability to weather the ups and downs of life are tied to your personal readiness. The amazing thing about this preparation is that everyone has the <u>*same*</u> *opportunity* to prove their response - ability. Notice that both foundations received the exact same encounters. Each had rain, floods, and wind, respectively. Both foundations had to prove their worth in a tangible way. I would go on record and say that it is only when storms hit do you fully test your preparation. If you are never tested by circumstances beyond your control, you will not get an accurate read on your capacity to rise up and win in the battle. Let me give you a tool to understand this better for real life. It is called PDCA and I will unpack what it means to you, personally.

PDCA is used in manufacturing worlds to assess current conditions and improve performance in the future. The P is for Plan. Improvement, like preparation, requires a plan of action. Nothing changes randomly, Absolutely Nothing! You must <u>create</u> a plan for a course of action to be implemented. Here is an example of such. At my place of employment, we do mock fire and tornado drills. Why? We are testing our preparedness for the real event. What about life? Do you do mock life situations and see how you would respond. Do you have a plan for life's windfalls?

The D is for Do. You must <u>work</u> the plan. Action is necessary at this point. You must perform the steps of your plan to the best of your ability. Perfection is not the goal here. Action is! When you become active, you begin to learn of your preparation and its capability in real-time events.

The C is for Check. <u>Measure</u> the outcome against the expected goal. How did you do? Did you hit the target? Where on the bullseye did your shot land? You need to know how you did in this setting. It is an indicator of your preparedness and what you learned about yourself during the mock drill.

The A is for Act. Action is required as you <u>adjust</u> the plan. Do a re-do. Check the results again. Then, act again! If you can't tell by now, this is a *cycle* that gets repeated, indefinitely. Why? Improvement and preparation are never ending propositions. *You can always improve your results in a repetitive manner.*

The PDCA of life is just as REAL, too. You must always be in a mode of improving, stretching, enhancing, and adding to your toolbox of life skills. It is by this means of advancing that you raise your hand in victory when the rains come, the flood rises, and the winds beat against your established home. Your foundation of preparation is the ace up your sleeve for life. With it, you can overcome the most difficult of events such as the death of a child, the loss of a job, the diagnosis of cancer, the financial strains of our economic day, the news of spousal infidelity, or the betrayal of a friend. No, these are not fun events, but they don't have to sink your boat when they show up.

Think back to a recent situation or event in your life. How prepared did you feel to handle it? Did you want to run and hide? Did you pretend it did not exist or deny its reality? Did you get angry and fight? What happened to make the details better or the outcome smoother? Anything? If you come to life's duel and you have no bullets in your gun, life will shoot you down and you will be the winner of lead vitamins. However, if by preparation, you load your gun, life will be left bent over as you make swiss cheese out of its attempt to sideline you. You can win. But, Personal Growth makes life *hard*.

Take just a minute and reflect on the four areas mentioned: *1. Relationships, 2. Debt Elimination, 3. Career Development, and 4. Personal Growth.* Which one jumps out at you as the stubbed toe? Maybe, there is more than one. Could it be that you have <u>never</u> considered these key areas until today and now understand that LIFE is waiting on you to get busy and ready yourself in this RDCP journey? No shortcuts here! Sweat, commitment, and determination must surface before we move forward in our discussion.

Now, if it were not enough to have to make each specific area of relationships, debt elimination, career development, and personal growth work on their own, try to manage them **all** at the same time. Yes, that's right, at the same time. Why? *Real life does not happen in a linear fashion. Life is coming at us as all four areas <u>collide</u> at <u>one</u> <u>time</u>.* You need to keep each area balanced and all four legs on the ground as shown in the stool above. Each leg needs to provide sustenance for your stool called *Life.* You need 100% participation from each supporting leg in order to sit comfortably on the stool.

This pictorial of the stool helps provide so much insight. You need this to reveal areas of weakness that must be shored up. For example, let's say for sake of illustration that you are 100% in relationships, debt elimination and career development, but only 75% in preparation. In this case, then, you are only balancing on 3 of the 4 legs of the stool. What extra effort is needed to balance on just three legs? Your lack of preparation will cause you to be unstable and overwork the other areas to keep from falling over. In this instance, preparation *must* be increased to bring balance to your world.

Now, what if you are 100% in debt elimination, career development, and personal growth, but only 65% in relational health. Once again, you can enjoy this for a time, but your lack of relational strength will ultimately strain the other areas and cause you to fail in your other solid areas. Your relational dynamics must be improved and given priority to bring the stool back in balance once again.

I am taking the time to explain these real-life possibilities because they shed light into our human tendency. When a particular area is difficult, we tend to migrate to the other areas of strength and think that if these are good, then I can live with a little less health and strength in another. We may even go so far as to ignore we have a problem in one particular area. Hitherto, the *complete* truth is your life will be unstable and unbalanced if all four legs are <u>not</u> squarely balanced on the floor called Life. *You can't pretend that all is well when it really is not.* Your stool will give you away and everything will point to unhealthy dynamics in one or more of the four areas.

Our collision insurance is the grace of God. In the heat of every single moment, life can get extremely wild. We may find ourselves reacting to situations and events, both within our control and out of our control, that cause collisions in our four key areas. Each day, there is movement in each of the four areas. Some days you are adding to the health of each area. On other days, you are deducting from the accounts of each. *This vacillation can be grueling and relentless.* God gives you the grace to keep life balanced and stable. Consider this verse from the Word of God as found in Romans 8:28 (CEB), [28] *We know that God works all things together for good for the ones who love God, for those who are called according to his purpose.* This verse is your <u>hope</u> for every day living. Why? You are going to have challenges balancing the four key areas. Some days you will feel like a winner and some days, you will walk away with your head hung low, feeling the sting of instability. Nevertheless, God's got your back and His provision will sustain you in the difficult seasons of life and transition. Life can be an enjoyable experience and in the next chapter, we will begin to explore how to make your life a masterpiece of epic proportions with ease.

It's Your Move!

1. Why is Life so hard? What are your initial thoughts?

   _____.

2. The four key areas do collide. Which ones impact you the most? Why? _____.

3. What steps can be taken to improve your growth area? a. _____

   b. _____

   c. _____

4. PDCA - Plan, Do, Check, Act: What mock test should you create and test? _____. List three ingredients needed for preparation success.

   a. _____

   b. _____

   c. _____

6

Your Turning Point

The year was 1979. The setting was Lawrenceville, Georgia. The place was Central Gwinnett High School. I would officially become a Black Knight, our school mascot. It was finally here. Years of physical growth and chronological age would surrender to my desires. I would be entering the ranks of becoming a high school student. No more being a child. I was becoming a young adult, a pre-man if you will. And, I liked it. Everyone dreams of entering high school as to believe this is the start of something *BIG*. Yes, I was growing up and I felt the weight of this moment. In four years, I would be deciding on a college direction and preparing for adulthood in a very authentic way. However, today, I was too excited to be thinking of graduation. I was just wanting to have some fun. Girls, pep rallies, high school dances, and dating were on my radar. I, like every generation before me, made out like high school was a permanent vacation. I could not wait to find out for myself.

I know what you're thinking, "What does that have to do with the title called Turning Points"? I am glad you asked. Turning Points! Two words, but with *powerful* implications. Have you ever had a turning point? I have! I am sure you have as well. In fact, I am still having turning points and I am certain you are too. Let me give you an example of a particular one I had in high school.

Algebra! Need I say more! This is one of those words that brings out intense sweating, mild confusion, and heart palpitations. It always produces flu-like symptoms. Algebra can do that to the best of students. It was here, Algebra. Now, let me take you back one year to my 8th grade math class. It was here that I was first introduced to Algebra (I finally learned it was not a bra that supported algae). Yet, during this year, I was completely focused on having fun and enjoying my weekends. I didn't study and I really didn't care about passing this class. In fact, I did poorly in the class and my parents knew that by virtue of periodic report cards. So, thankfully, I convinced my father, over the summer, to take Algebra over again, but this time take it in two parts, Part 1 and Part 2. Basically, you take two years to cover this material rather than one. Yeah! I was going to have an easy math ride for my first two years in high school. How cool is that? I thought I had pulled a fast one on everybody.

Day 1 of high school, my math teacher learned that I had taken Algebra while in 8th grade and advised that I should try it again. What? I didn't want to try it again. She gave me a few days to decide and said the decision was totally up to me. In those few days, *I had a Turning Point*. If I were honest with myself, I did not apply my best study habits to the subject of Algebra. Truthfully, I did not give an honest effort to this subject. I really did not do it justice and it was not Algebra's fault. *It was mine!* There, I said it. I feel so much better now! Confession is good for the soul. I went back to Mrs. Johnson and told her I was in - and away I went on this Algebra roller coaster. I promised her I would do my best and if I needed help, I would come to her for extra time to master this subject (if it can be mastered at all). Much to my surprise, I was starting to connect the dots. It wasn't so hard after all. I began to somewhat like Algebra. In fact, I began to like math, in general. It began to click with me.

Day-after-day, month-after-month, I applied my efforts to learning Algebra. To my amazement, I was even asked to join the math team for the school. Really? How could this be? The math team for the Black Knights? Not me! While I did help them out from time to time, I didn't aspire to join, but the fact that they saw this potential in me was encouraging. As the school year marched to a close, we had our annual awards day. As usual, they announced names of those who surpassed everyone's expectations and were crowned Mr. Chemistry and Miss English. When it came time for the math awards to be dished out, I was shocked to hear my named called out for Mr. Algebra. Me? Mr. Algebra? No way! They went on to explain that I had the highest-grade point average (GPA) of any of the algebra students and therefore, I was awarded the school's Algebra Award. I still have that certificate to this day, over 30 years later. It is a reminder of a Turning Point in my life.

Let me share another significant Turning Point for me. The Algebra Award really messed me up because I had never won anything before. *It showed me what effort, determination, and commitment can do in any given area of life, after a __REAL__ Turning Point has finally been made.*

Let me dial in on another area that God was working on while in high school. It was one of great importance to me: *my identity.* As I mentioned earlier, my 8th grade year was all about having fun and weekend activity. I had fallen into the wrong crowd and I began to experiment with alcohol and low octane drugs like marijuana. All drugs are bad, I know. However, I was scared to death of big drugs like cocaine and heroin. I stayed far away from those during my high school years. In any event, I found myself in a very peculiar high school mix. I would hang out with those who had leather jackets, smoked cigarettes, and partied a lot, even before school started. Yet, academically, I was in all the college preparation classes with those who looked quite studious and brainy. Here's my identity crisis in full swing. I ran with a rough crowd, but studied with a nerdy bunch. I was in classes with "A" students and I would hear the conversations of those who were glad to get a "D" on a test. It got to the point with my bro's that I did not discuss my grades for fear of ridicule and being labeled a book worm.

Another factor was that I would go to all the concerts with the boys and drink and have a great time. In those days, I would be labeled a head banger because I listened to groups like AC/DC, Iron Maiden, Judas Priest, Ozzy, Ratt, and Poison. It was called the metal band era of the 80's. Don't get me wrong. I also listened to groups like Bon Jovi, Journey, Foreigner, Styx, and Eddie Money. They were rock bands, but were more main stream and accepted in most circles. I just enjoyed music and every style allowed me to learn more about the drums and for that I was grateful. I was known in high school as the Drummer man because I played for most of the football pep rallies and often got to do solos which people liked. *It was my own brand of infant fame, so to speak.*

In addition, I was the guy who would camp out for concert tickets and wait in line all night for the best seats, front row if possible. I took everyone's order and would buy the maximum amount of tickets allowed. It was a blast for me to camp out with other like-minded concert goers. We would play the artist's music, blasting from the back of someone's car speakers. We would talk about seeing them last year and what we liked about the latest album release (yes, I said album). I took pleasure in going to concerts because I adored being a musician myself, a drummer boy. (The Little Drummer Boy was my favorite Christmas song. Just so you know?)

In my era, artists produced a record every year and toured to support their music. In that period, you had to buy the whole album and like every song or skip past it on the album while listening by lifting up the needle and literally placing it on the next song. Yes, times were tough back then, I know. No iTunes or CD's, back then. Just good, old-fashioned vinyl. In any event, I was known at school as the concert guy, Mr. Head Banger, the Drummer man, the Leather-jacket crowd, and the Beta Club member, the Honor Roll society guy, the Award grabber, and Mr. Brain. I had one foot on academics and a budding future and one foot on my wild identity and a party lifestyle. *I was miserable inside and tired of this tug-o-war lifestyle. Something needed to change.*

I can remember it vividly as God began to get my attention. It was during my 11th grade year that I was invited to church, with a substitute teacher, in downtown Atlanta. My parents agreed to allow me to attend and considered it okay to miss our home church activities. Yes, I did attend church often. I know I was not the best at living out what I was learning. However, all that was about to change. As mentioned, Mr. Jones (not his real name) took me and the high school quarterback, James, to church. We rode about 45 minutes into the big city of Atlanta, from Lawrenceville, and were excited to attend a large church setting. It was quite different than what I was used to seeing as people worshiped God. Yes, people were actually worshiping. At one point during the worship time, I saw Mr. Jones with tears in his eyes. I just stared, at times, for a moment. He was crying and I was moved inside. This God had an impact on his life in a tangible way. He was engaging His God and it was not just about behavior modification or moral standards. Mr. Jones loved God and I felt his deep devotion, first hand. He helped me greatly that day.

At the same time, I met a young man in my advanced placement history class named John. John and I hit it off and we became instant friends. He and I were like two peas in a pod as they say and I really needed a friend like him. Yes, he knew I was a rock-n-roller, but he didn't care. Yes, he knew I had the leather jacket. He didn't care. Yes, he knew I partied on the weekends. He didn't care. He liked me for simply being me. Then, one day I was invited to have lunch with his family. I accepted and found myself in the middle of a holy-rolling bunch. Well, not really! They just loved God too, in a noticeable way and, this time, I had access to their lives on a daily basis as John and I became Best Friends. We still are to this day, over three decades!

John's dad conducted a Friday night Bible Study and I was invited to attend. What? Give up my Friday nights to learn about God? *Turning Points are not always easy or predictable, I must say.* Yes, I began to attend these weekly studies and my life was in transition toward God. I felt loved, valued, and accepted in our Bible study group. We learned about the grace and mercy of a Heavenly Father who could wipe away your past and give you a fresh start and a new identity in Jesus Christ. My heart resonated with this message and I wanted to know God in this way. I attended this study for the rest of my high school years and into college. From 1982 to 1986, I made Friday nights a time of learning about a God who could change your life from the inside out and make you into a new person. *How refreshing and cleansing, all at the same time.*

I can remember in 1986 my most important Turning Point. I made Jesus Christ the <u>Master</u> (Lord as is often stated) of my life and I yielded my heart to Him in every way. Notice, it took almost 4 years of weekly study and interaction with Believers for me to completely <u>surrender</u> (trust) my mind, will, and emotion to Jesus Christ. This Turning Point was a process as I actively pursued the God of the Bible. It was different than simply attending church, or being good, or saying a blessing before a meal, or caring for the poor. I, now, had a one-on-one relationship with the God of the Universe. I was His child and He was now my Heavenly Father. I have actively engaged in this relationship now for over three decades and day-by-day, I am being made more like Him. *Note that this Turning point was really a slow journey.* The day I said yes to Jesus was the actual Turning Point for a life of purpose, passion, and peace.

If you would be so kind, please allow me to share one final turning point that may help illustrate this point even further. The previous turning points, while difficult at the time, only involved me in its scope of impact. What do you do with Turning Points that affect others, like your family, in countless ways? That is a good question and to be honest, the lion's share of turning points do affect other people as well. I will share a story of my own that will help to unlock this principle even further. The details ahead are real, raw, and representative of life's trying moments.

Joblessness – the true test of male humanity. Have you been there? It looms as a monster. It stalks the best of men, wanting to leave you vulnerable and open to screams of doubt, discouragement, and fear. Do you know this insidious mammoth? I do, all too well. I spent most of my life as an over-achiever and I was grateful for the work ethic I was taught growing up from both of my parents. I was certainly *not* afraid to put in a full day's work and enjoyed the fruit of my labors. However, when I was struck with a period of joblessness, I can't begin to tell you how it impacted my physical health, mental health, and outlook on life. When I made a move for my family to be closer to relatives and immediate circles of influence, I left a great job in Columbia, SC to move back to Athens, Georgia. Now, for the first time, I didn't leave a job for another job. I resigned on my own with the *belief* that I would quickly find a comparable job in my new place of residence (Note: at the time, in 2002, my wife had already landed a job at a local hospital). Because I had always had gainful employment, I did not truly fear finding a job replacement. How hard could that be? My thoughts were always positive and my expectations high. I polished up my resume and prepared to send out many. In the college town where we landed, Athens, Georgia, there were very few manufacturing companies to speak of (I learned that the hard way). This Georgia Bulldog home had much to offer the rising family in terms of education, recreation, and community (and hospitals for my wife's employment), but the likes of a Mechanical Design Engineering job were nowhere to be found. I, literally, sent out hundreds of resumes over a four-year period, 2002 to 2006 to find an engineering position. Nonetheless, as time marched on, I sent them to organizations like the Girl Scouts of America to Tru-Green Lawn Care, and everything in between. My widening, job willingness circle was growing as well as the radius I was willing to travel for any type of technical employment, or employment at all for that matter. I did a brief spell with the Boy Scouts of America (about 30 days) and realized my world of Eagle Scout living was minimal. While I needed a job, this one was not a career fit or a family-friendly fit for that matter. For this brief experience, I was never at home while fulfilling the duties of this job. As it turned out, I did step away from this job opportunity and continued my resume expedition.

As the years began to fly by, the spirt of my heart, as a Man and Provider, began to die, too. Sleeplessness, anxiety, and depression were awaiting to jump on me like a lion in a jungle full of antelope. I was frantic to land <u>something</u> to provide for my family. In a last-ditch attempt, I did land a job working with granite and kitchen designs as a drafter, as mentioned earlier. Not what I had in mind, for sure! Not the pay either, but I was grateful to see someone was interested in me as an employee. It felt good to be wanted! *A Turning Point had finally arrived!*

As you would expect, we all have *Turning Points*, that moment when the *desire* and *decision* for change converge. Notice, I said desire and decision. Desire always proceeds decision. *Nothing happens without the desire for change.* Turning Points don't occur without desire. No one <u>ever</u> stumbled into a Turning Point. Desire is stirring long before every turning point. However, desire is <u>not</u> enough. Decision must follow desire. There must be a deciding moment, a turning point, for change. I like to think of it as a stake in the road. A marker. A stone of remembrance. A point of change. Turning Points have power.

They ignite the soul and bolster the human spirit. Life shapes itself by Turning Points. They are not always easy, free, or cheap. Turning Points have a cost. Comfort, reputation, security, identity, and will all must _bow_ to Turning Points. Yet, I would not have it any other way. _Turning Points create life. Turning Points create HOPE, too._

What about you? Have you ever experienced a Turning Point? Do you ever desire a turning point? What comes to mind? As noted earlier, desire and decision are paramount for turning points to occur. Maybe, the first step is praying for a desire to change a particular area of your life. Decisions always follow desire. Do you have the desire, but are afraid to plan for fear of the outcome? I understand! Turning Points do not come willingly. They _never_ just yield to change. No! Turning Points rise out of the smoke of the battle. Turning Points come with a fight, a persistent fight! The ashes of yesterday are the seeds of Turning Points for your tomorrow. _Victory is defined by Turning Points in the mind followed by activity in the natural._ Engage your present and thus strengthen your future. If you allow it, _Turning Points change everything._ Your Turning Point awaits!

Let me give you one last piece of encouragement before we launch into the next chapter. Not everyone will be excited about your turning points. Some folks just like you the way you are. Some people are glad you are average so they can feel good about their own inactivity and lack of change. What? Are you telling me that others will scoff and ridicule my desire and decision for more in my life? _That is exactly what I am saying to you._ No one who ever sets out for change has a line of individuals applauding his or her efforts on the road to somewhere. _That is just the way life is._ When I was growing up there was a popular song called "Misery Loves Company". Need I say more. There is a continual feast at the table of mediocrity and when you decide to leave that table and set out for a new dining experience, others will try to talk you out of it and / or will talk about you when you exit. _They really will, every time._ You will hear ALL the reasons to play it safe.

You will learn of the dangers of change. You will be convinced that where you are is really not that bad and, in fact, we have been here for generations and it has served our family lineage well. Why do you want to go and rock the boat, any way? Most of these informants will be in your *own family and your very closest friends.* They will be confident that they are seeking to protect you. In the end, they are preventing a future Turning Point. Respect the person and the opinion he or she may offer, *but launch out into the deep, no matter the chatter!*

It's Your Move!

1. Turning Points? To date, what has been your most significant one? _____.

2. What three things can you do to improve your desire for Turning Points? a. _____.

   b. _____.

   c. _____.

3. What two decisions do you need to make today to create a Turning Point? a. _____.

   b. _____.

4. Identity was a BIG one for me. On a scale from 0 (low) to 10 (high), do you struggle with identity?

   0 _____ 5 _____ 10

5. List some ways you can settle your identity question in the way God views you? Read John 3:16! You are that valuable. _____

7

Truths, Tools, and Time

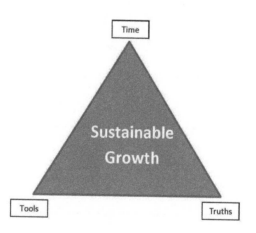

This chapter will excite your inner being because I begin to share ways to grow, engage, and stretch for new life. As you might expect, nothing prepares you for a better tomorrow like understanding this chapter's content. Truths, Tools, and Time will be the buzz words to make Turning Points a permanent reality in your life. It is also

Truths, Tools, and Time that will be the anchor to keep you focused on tomorrow when the desire to go back to the familiar is easier than the *effort* of creating the new. Been there - done that and I have the scars to prove it. In any event, your emerging life is waiting under the covering of Truths, Tools, and Time. Let's look at each one individually and then put them back together near the end of this chapter to see their impact on your life.

Truths — Everything starts with truth! Not just any truth, but Biblical Truth. *I know that sounds a little old fashioned and out-dated, but there must be a Rock against which everything can be tried and tested and stand firm in the end.* For me, that Rock is Jesus Christ, the Son of the Living God. Jesus said this about himself as found in John 14:6, "Jesus answered, I am the way, the truth, and the life. No one comes to the Father except through me." (CEB). For me, the Word of God is <u>MY</u> Anchor? *What about your life?* What truth sustains you in turbulent times? In life, you must have an anchor, fixed and unmovable, which will hold you during the storms, floods, and winds of reality. You can *bet* the farm that they're coming and coming with power to ruin your life. The Bible even paints this picture to meditate on as found in I Peter 5: 8, "Be clearheaded. Keep alert. Your accuser, the devil, *is on the prowl like a roaring lion,* seeking someone to devour." (CEB). Don't worry! I am not an alarmist, painting a doom and gloom picture. However, I do want you to be *realistic* and know that you <u>do</u> have an enemy working to destroy your life. *He is unyielding and fierce.*

Absolute Truth, as found in the Bible, gives you the basis or foundation for change. Let me give you a real-life example. If your marriage is less than exciting, joyful and fulfilling, there is an underlying dynamic creating this condition. What if the Bible gives you two Truth Bricks as found in Ephesians 5:33, "In any case, as for you individually, each one of you (men) should love his wife as himself, and wives (women) should respect their husbands." (CEB). This Truth is found by stating, Men, "Love your wife as you love yourself, daily and wholeheartedly." Ladies, "Make sure you always show <u>proper</u> respect to your husband, lovingly and sincerely." Why? A Woman's # I need is security as found in a constant, loving relationship. Additionally, a Man's # I need is honor as shown by proper respect for his role as head of the home (God said it and I'm just repeating it). These two Truths can revolutionize your marriage bond. They are constants or *Absolute Truths* in a world filled with shifting truths. These two ingredients will fill your marriage with hope, promise, and longevity. Consequently, they never go out of style. As you can see, Truth paves the way for abundant living, effective and fruitful in every way.

Tools – If Truths provide the "Why" for change, the Tools provide the "How" for change. Everyone likes tools. Why? Because tools make life easier and we like our lives to be **easy**. Yes, the right tool for the right job proves to be a time saver and a game changer. Take any random tool box in Hometown, USA. You may find a hammer, a screw driver (Philips and Flat Head), a pair of pliers, a level, a tape measure, and an adjustable wrench. What comes to mind as I mention each of the tools? *How about the function it performs!* When the word hammer comes into play, you don't think of taking measurements do you? Of course not, you think of pounding and banging. What if I mention the word, level, do you think of tightening a nut on a bolt. I sure hope not! You think of making something parallel to the floor in your home or building a wall that is a perfect 90° to its adjoining member. Without a doubt, *the tool defines the function it performs and the outcome it creates.* You can sit back and look at the beauty of a picture that is perfectly level above your couch. You can see your handy work as outlined by a screw driver when you connect two pieces together. Here is the best part. *No tool becomes obsolete in a matter of years or with each changing societal awareness.* Hammers will always be hammers. Pliers will always be pliers. Tape Measures will always be measurement devices. Why? Tools provide lasting functions, no matter the setting, season, or society. A hammer in China will do the exact same work as a hammer in India or New York City. Tools are designed that way and we like it. *They are constants!*

Not to be overlooked in the tool department by men, women love tools too, just in a different arena. Take for example Mixers from heaven, as shown on QVC, that has every attachment ever invented. *It does "everything" for you.* Why, even the bowl spins on its own. Yes, having to expend movement from your arm to create a rotational motion is so old school. Mixers today will give you the benefit of making breads, pastries, cakes, and various other delightful dishes with ease. It's a multi-tasking dream for the modern woman.

What about the food processor? I am here to tell you that food processors are divine gifts from God. In moments, you get things cut up as fine as your heart desires. My wife owns the *"Ninja"*. Even the name sounds like an Asian special forces team, coming into our kitchen, to perform some kung-fu, kitchen martial arts. The *Ninja* will cut metal if you are not careful and certainly a finger if you are not paying attention. This tool should have a warning label for the newbie kitchen apprentice.

Finally, the electric can opener. How many years have women lost opening cans with a manual opener. Ladies, I feel your pain in a very real way. You have better things to do than slowly open cans of green beans, peaches, or soup. Babies are crying. Clothes to be washed are calling. And, the dish washer is needing affection and affirmation! Your love of tools is combined with your ability to just get things done, quickly and often. Your output with a gadget trumps a great day with a manual tool any day of the week. So, it is for ladies!

What about Tools for *effective* and *efficient* living? Do they offer the same universality and benefits? A resounding YES! Let me take a minute and expound on the above two words as it pertains to every day outcomes. Effectiveness is often linked to the concept of doing something that is *best*. The output is purposeful, impactful, and life-changing. Effectiveness is important to the manufacturing world because you want to know that you are doing the best things for the company for effective growth. Efficiency, on the other hand, is defined as *best practices*. The underlying thought is "Am I maximizing my efforts to create the best outcome in the fewest steps possible?" No wasted motion, time, or processes, etc. is the mark of an efficient task. Marry effectiveness with efficiency and you have a knock out combination. I have heard it stated this way for clarity, "Efficiency is doing things right (managerial stuff) while effectiveness is doing the right things (leadership stuff)."

These two words, together, can often be found in the world of Lean manufacturing, a Toyota method of creating saleable goods such as cars. The *big* emphasis is on eliminating *Waste* (things that add cost, but no real apparent value) as found in the following acronym: TIMWOOD

- Transportation
- Inventory
- Motion
- Waiting
- Over Processing
- Over Producing
- Defects

Before you bury your head in the pillow you are laying upon because of my technical information overload, this stuff has tremendous significance for your every day life. Let me explain! You want to have the best possible life outcomes, yielding a lasting legacy and present-tense blessings. Everyone does and I am in the same line with you. However, if you don't know what is stealing or wasting your joy, peace, and passion, *you will continue to walk in discouragement, doubt, and defeat.*

Here is an additional approach to think about for what I want you to learn in this chapter about Tools. A second way to describe a Tool is defined by a single element: *Application*. In other words, if I know the Truth about a thing, but don't have the tools or ability to apply or work that truth, then I become frustrated, extremely frustrated. Here is the best way to make this stick in your life. I developed this phrase or motto over 25 years ago <u>AND</u> it still applies perfectly today:

Information (Truth) without Application (Tools) leads to <u>Frustration</u> and therefore, <u>Stagnation</u>.

vs.

Information (Truth) with Application (Tools) leads to <u>Expectation</u>, and therefore, <u>Transformation</u>.

Tools give you the ability to work out the Truth in your day-to-day settings with patience and promise. Here is a tangible way to exercise this learning principle. Read Psalm 1 below:

Psalm 1 (CEB)

*1 The truly happy person
doesn't follow wicked advice,
doesn't stand on the road of sinners,
and doesn't sit with the disrespectful.
² Instead of doing those things,
these persons love the LORD's Instruction,
and they recite God's Instruction day and night!
³ They are like a tree replanted by streams of water,
which bears fruit at just the right time
and whose leaves don't fade.
Whatever they do succeeds.*

⁴ That's not true for the wicked!
They are like dust that the wind blows away.
⁵ And that's why the wicked will have no standing in the court of justice—

neither will sinners
in the assembly of the righteous.
⁶ The LORD is intimately acquainted
with the way of the righteous,
but the way of the wicked is destroyed.

What *TOOLS* jump out at you while reading these verses? How about this one, *"The Lord's instructions will help me be successful in my every day living and I will be a person who bears fruit (outcomes) at just the right time in my life."* Therefore, if I set aside time to know God's Word, I can expect a life-time of fruit (blessings, not necessarily money) to come into my life. This is a "hammer" for effective and efficient living and this hammer is the same in every season, setting, and society of life. This tool can be trusted and the working of this tool produces a life filled with excitement, expectation, and peace.

Here is a second *TOOL* as found in the above verses, *"Who you run with will determine where life takes you and if the outcome is potentially disastrous."* You must work this tool as well. Be mindful of who you let into your inner circle. The company you keep will determine the quality and direction of your life. Like begets like as the book of Genesis confirms. The Bible gives a stern warning as found in I Corinthians 15:53, *"Do not be deceived, bad company corrupts good character."* This is **so** true and this tool applies the same in the United States, Russia, Japan, or even Trinidad where Lorraine is from! I heard one leadership expert say that you are the average of the five people you spend the most time with. Think about that for a minute. What would this average flesh out to be like? Uplifting? Determined? Courageous? Compassionate? These are in the good arena. What about the harmful side? What if the average characteristics are as follows: Lazy? Unloving? Liar?

Jealous? Angry? You can't afford to have these ingredients bombarding your life or your inner circle.

I hope you are getting the picture of tools and their great benefits to your life. They are useful and productive!

Time – Change needs time. Yes, it does! Not only the investment of your time, but also the passage of chronological time. Some things simply can not be rushed. You can plant a seed in the ground today and tomorrow it will <u>not</u> have a sprout on it. Why? It takes time for things to grow. You understand this intuitively, but it is hard to internalize in the thick of things.

Your first priority is to invest time into change initiatives. Whether it is to begin a degree at a local college, build a small business, get your body in shape or improve your marriage and relationship with your children, you have to give up small amounts of pre-committed time to the new agenda. *Time will not find you. NO, you must find time!* It will require diligence and effort on your part to carve out time. As I am writing this chapter, I am sitting here in silence in the comfort of my own home, at 6:30 am. Guess what? There is <u>no</u> activity at this hour of the morning that will interrupt my plans to write this book. However, I can think of a million reasons to be back in my warm bed, getting some extra Monday morning sleep. My will to write has trumped my desire to sleep in. Therefore, these pages today are a result of a hard-fought battle for my *time.* What I choose to do daily, with my time, will determine my future quality of life and destiny. It will not come easy and there will be a death to some things that once had a higher priority. TIME is necessary for lasting change and you *must* be willing to invest for your future state. *It is well worth it in the end!*

In addition to your investment of time, you will also need the passage of time. In my above description of a college degree, you will have to invest daily amounts of energy to finish each class. Finishing one class at a time is wonderful and you will grow with each one. Nevertheless, if your career aspiration is to have a Bachelor's degree, you have a number of classes to complete and that will require a plan and years of time. You can't take an inordinate number of classes, hoping to expedite your graduation goals. No! You have to register each semester and take a _reasonable_ number of classes in the context of your responsibilities and present world. Day-by-day, and week-by-week, and month-by-month, and year-by-year, you advance in change. The Bible calls these blocks of time, _seasons_. Seasons are prescribed amounts of time in which something is living. There is a time for everything under the sun as spoken by Solomon, declared to be the wisest man who ever lived next to Jesus Christ. This truth is spoken so beautifully as found in Ecclesiastes 3:1 – 8 (CEB),

There's a season for everything
and a time for every matter under the heavens:
² a time for giving birth and a time for dying,
a time for planting and a time for uprooting what was planted,
³ a time for killing and a time for healing,
a time for tearing down and a time for building up,
⁴ a time for crying and a time for laughing,
a time for mourning and a time for dancing,
⁵ a time for throwing stones and a time for gathering stones,
a time for embracing and a time for avoiding embraces,
⁶ a time for searching and a time for losing,
a time for keeping and a time for throwing away,
⁷ a time for tearing and a time for repairing,
a time for keeping silent and a time for speaking,
⁸ a time for loving and a time for hating,
a time for war and a time for peace.

These verses spell out a profound truth and can be a tool for you in the progression of change. *Notice that life has movement associated with it.* Hence, your life has movement as well. This movement is crucial to the advancement of growth, purpose, and expectation. Your awareness of this movement will help you *relax* and enjoy the journey. Some things can't be rushed and if you received it prematurely, you would not be able to handle it, anyway. Maturity, development, growth, and progress can't be fast-tracked because you simply want it quicker. Let it grow, naturally. *And, you'll be glad you waited for it.*

As you begin to converge the ingredients of Truths, Tools, and Time, the chemistry of these will create an <u>explosion</u> in your life, for good. I like to call this the "TNT" for explosive living. Truths and Tools are the rudimentary ingredients. Add in a little Time, and you will see the effects of your efforts as you traffic through life with its Rugged Terrain agenda. With these crucial, building blocks, we can advance forward, taking on *anything* that crosses our paths. As we move into the next chapter, we will reference the nuggets of gold learned in this chapter.

It's Your Move!

1. Tools! What is your favorite tool? Why? Could you live without it? _____

    _____.

2. Truths! What is your Anchor for lasting Truth? Do you look to God's Word for divine Truth? Why or why not?

    _____

    _____.

3. Time! Do you invest time into your personal growth? Are you frustrated because growth seems slow? List two ways to get more time to grow. _____

    _____.

4. Life is made of seasons. What season are you in? _____

    _____.

5. Will you commit to daily read God's Word to grow?

8

The Uncharted Dynamics of Life

My former employer, at the time of this writing, encouraged every employee to give a minimum of two hours of community service to charitable organizations to fulfill one of its core values of *social responsibility*. While serving in mid-July of 2014, I met a young girl whose name was Sam. She and I were volunteering with our company at a local soup kitchen for the homeless. Sam was a wide-eyed, bright Asian student with big dreams and whimsical ideas. She was the daughter of one of my co-workers. I was fascinated with her passion for life at such a young age.

Seeking to make small talk with her as we wrapped a set of utensils around a napkin, I asked her what grade she was in. She quickly confirmed that she was a Junior in high school. I further delved into her world and asked if she had given any consideration to her future career aspiration, including a college interest. She perked up and told me *"I already have my life mapped out!"* That statement brought a smile to my face as I listened intently. I pondered her thoughts as she proceeded to share *exactly* how life was going to unfold for her. She went on to tell me <u>what</u> will happen and <u>when</u> it is going to happen. Almost like a recipe, she added each ingredient of life and began to mix up the batter for a cake all of us would love to eat. The dental hygienist career will allow her to only work 16 days out of each month as most work Monday to Thursday. This would give her time to start a family and invest in her children's school activities. Her free time would be used to keep up her home and invest in her marital success. I must say she had it all *figured* out and her *mental picture* of life was a work of art in the making. I can't imagine with that much thought and passion why she would not look forward with great expectation, promise, and joy. *Who wouldn't love what she had in mind!*

As she concluded the details of her *perfect* life and our service to the homeless had ended, I wished her well in her pursuits and told her to follow her dreams. She gave a courteous smile back at me and then headed down the walkway toward her car with her dad by her side. I though to myself as we parted, *"Life is uncharted"*. You may wish your journey is that textbook in nature, but what actually occurs is far from planned.

The *"Uncharted Dynamics of Life!* Does it grab your attention? Much like my new friend, Sam, you can plan until your heart's content what life is *supposed* to look like. We all do that. Yet, Life is <u>not</u> this way. No guides, no experts leading the way, no master script to follow, just 24/7 navigation through choppy and pounding waters. Let me illuminate this in a very tangible way. This is a true story and one which should bring a chuckle inside. My vulnerability will serve to be humorous.

Growing up in Buffalo, NY, I had never been to the beach. Yes, we lived near Lake Erie which is far from the ideals of the lakes near my new home in Georgia. I had always heard of beach excitement and wanted to eventually go to the ocean. One year after moving to Georgia, I made friends with a young fellow named Tim who took an annual pilgrimage to Panama City Beach. I questioned him on the details of pretty girls in bikinis and sunset scenes of beach living. Yes, I was only <u>thirteen</u> at the time so girls and fun were my *BIG* thoughts for the day. I was definitely intrigued by the information Tim shared and dreamed of the day when, I too, could experience the sand in my toes and fruit drinks by the crashing waves and, the girls in two-piece bikinis. What can I say? Boys will be boys. I was 100% male at 13 years of age.

The annual trip was forthcoming and to my excitement, Tim asked if I wanted to go with him. He was allowed to invite one friend each year, as was his sister, and this year was my big break. I was the chosen one and I was a little nervous if I had to be completely honest. In fact, I had never really traveled that far from home or away from my parents so this trip was quite a stretch out of my comfort zone. I was willing and counted down the days to the ultimate vacation.

While on the drive down, I learned that Tim and his family did an annual deep-sea fishing day. An eight-hour, chartered trip with an *Expert of the Sea* sounded different than my fishing off the bank days back home in Buffalo. I would be out in the ocean, far from everything with <u>no</u> land in sight. I would be catching fish that makes you want to capture the memory on film. What could be better than that? My "mental picture" was of a perfect day, a memorable snap shot in time. My enthusiasm was building as we enjoyed each day leading up to this fishing excursion.

The morning finally arrived and I was up at the crack of dawn, dreaming of this *Kodak* moment (I know I am dating my self, but that is what we used to say). I wanted to catch the biggest fish and share this event with my family back in Georgia. The family piled in the boat at 6 am, bringing our breakfast on the boat to save some time for fishing. We gobbled down our food as we sailed out to the best fishing places. *Let's face it, that is why you hire a chartered expert.* You pay good money for his expertise and knowledge of the waters. The ocean was a majestic snapshot of God's creation and the likes of which I had yet to see in my young adult life. This is the stuff of which dreams are made of. Right? Right! Right.

Not too long into our trip, things began to change, for me that is! Yes, I was the newbie onboard in a boat full of expert fisherman. My first-time sea experience was beginning to tell on itself. Why would my fellow patrons _not_ inform me about the _realities_ of the sea? <u>Motion Sickness!</u> A robber of fishing dreams. A destroyer of vacation bliss. A devil of recreational paradise. A detriment to life itself. The sky didn't seem as blue anymore. The sun was not as bright as I remembered it while starting out. My life was coming to an end…or so I thought.

Yes, I said _"motion sickness"_. I had my pole in the water. The wind was in my hair. The boat was trolling along as we fished for monsters of the sea. I was having the time of my life, until a twinge of nausea surfaced. Wow! Maybe, I am just nervous about catching a big fish and being able to reel it in. I shrugged it off and ignored it's call. Like a fly buzzing around your meal at the family reunion, the feelings of motion sickness were looming. I soon couldn't concentrate if my pole was bending or not. In fact, I was becoming less interested by the second. I began to panic a bit. "Am I about to vomit?" Thoughts of embarrassment swirled around my head. I was hours from home, parents, familiar surrounds, and security. As luck would have it, I was about to lose my breakfast, dignity, afternoon, and memory. O joy of joys! Why Me, Lord?

I dodged the mammoth no longer. It was here. The vengeance of the sea monster pounced on me like a bandit in rage. Yes, I found myself getting very acquainted with the side of the boat. Not once, but for the next several hours. I would describe the experience as deathly. I wanted to die. I really wanted to die! Nausea, vomiting, weariness, sweating, and confusion, _all day long._ As I mentioned earlier, this was an eight-hour chartered trip. No cutting the day short for the wimpy new-comer who can't keep down his breakfast. Sympathy sure. Compassion, yes. But, "we've got fish to catch" was the motto for the day. I finally found a bed to lay down on after I lost my innards to this sea host. It was there that the ocean stopped spinning and the nausea gave me some peace. I found myself fast asleep. The motion of the ocean didn't bother me after I zonked out. I slept the <u>rest</u> of the trip. Oblivious to the fun the rest of the crowd was having. *I missed it.* And, I missed out. No Kodak moments. No fishing pictures to hang on my wall. No memorable stories to tell my grandchildren. No tales of the one that got away. My take away from the sea trip: vomit, sickness, sleep, nightmare. Sea Sickness torment at its best. There, I said it! This torment was an absolute fact.

Once again, let's transfer this mantra to REAL life. You have a "mental picture" of your life, just like I had a mental picture of this exquisite fishing trip. You prepare and plan for the ultimate outcome. You execute it with flawless perfection, given to specifics and timeliness. BAM, POW, SMACK. The outcome's shaky. The details fuzzy. The intent questioned. The results marginal. *What just happened?* Frustrated, angered, and wondering, you scratch your head and sigh! Every thought turns to reflection. "What went wrong? I planned this out with such skill and insight". Guess What? Everyone does! You are not alone here. Life is…Uncharted, Unpredictable, Unrelenting, Unfriendly! 24/7 x 365 days a year. It happens! And, it happens to the best of us.

What about your journey in life? Do you find yourself puzzled at life's outcomes? Do your chartered trips quickly become uncharted in nature, leaving you on the side of your proverbial boat while clutching the sides as you wish the trip would end? Do you ever wonder how you ended up <u>here</u> or <u>there</u>? Is the stress of your challenges eating into the pie of joy that you long for? We can all relate. *Life is unscripted and raw, at times.* It leaves little room for comfort, care, and compassion. It marches forward with the beat of the conga drums, deafening as it makes its way along the roads of reality.

Ironically, no one in *my* boat story told me about sea sickness or its potential effects. What? They were the experts of the sea. Knowledgeable, mature, seasoned, able. They knew the motion of the ocean can cripple a new-comer if he or she does not prepare for the journey. Yet, they remained silent as we boarded the boat. *Life will REMAIN silent, too.* No fanfare, no fore-warning, no emergency broadcast alerts. No Mama promptings. *LIFE*...Nothing quite prepares you for <u>this</u> trip. Your journey has potential. My sea trip did as well. *Study Life.* *Be Determined.* Look for the unexpected. Do your homework! Uncharted...Yes. Unproductive...That's your choice!

As we turn the corner and begin to formulate a strategy to overcome life's challenges and trying moments, we will understand more of who God created us to be and our ability to live above our present-day dynamics. Let's move on to Chapter 9.

It's Your Move!

I. "I've got my life all mapped out!" Like Sam, do you have a mental picture of your "perfect" life? _____ _____.

2. Is your life going as planned? Why or Why not? _____ _____ _____.

3. List two steps you can take to foster a more realistic idea about your life. a. _____. b. _____.

4. God knows your life from end to beginning. Will you begin to allow Him to guide you? Why or Why not? _____ _____.

5. Life is uncharted! Build into your days two buffers to win at life. a. _____ b. _____.

9

Precious Metals

Metals. Hmm. No, my friend, I entitled it "Precious Metals!" Please don't edit out the adjective here. Mere metals don't get noticed. As you would imagine, only precious metals get second *glances* and *chances.* You heard that right! *You are precious to God in every way!* Let me illustrate.

In the fall of each year, college students from every walk of life head off to college to advance their learning and career potential. My year was 1984. Stop laughing. I know that seems like ages ago and it was. Yes, I have made it to the Wisdom Club at my local church, 50 years old and above. I digress. Now, back to my story we go. The school setting is *Southern Polytechnic State University* (now part of Kennesaw State University) in Marietta, Georgia. The career of choice: mechanical engineering. You heard that right. Design, manufacturing, material calculations, stress analysis, fatigue studies, and 3-D modeling. My material of Choice: Metals, all types and sizes. Sound romantic? Not! But needed.

I have spent over 30 years of my mechanical engineering career working with metals and metal processes: bending, forming, welding, machining, grinding, casting, forging, shaping, etc. My father before me, a tool and die machinist by trade, spent his whole life working with metals, at his work and in our garage. As a result, over my 50+ year life span thus far, I have been saturated in the science and study of working with metals. Not a very dazzling medium I must confess, but essential in every sector of society. Metals are used in cars, buildings, bridges, machinery, guard rails, air planes, home appliances, computers, glasses, nail clippers, and batteries, etc. Yes, metals are everywhere and in everything. Just take a look around. You'll see what I am talking about!

I remember sitting in chemistry class, early one morning, having to learn the periodic table of elements. Metals have four main classes as I discovered. These classes include alkali metals, alkaline earth metals, transitional metals and other metals. My brain was about to explode as I tried to master metals of every kind. That's what Mechanical Engineers do! We are experts at metals and the means by which metals can be beneficial.

Guess what? I am not alone with my fascination with metals. The world over is mining for metals. Every type gets mined: iron ore, copper, gold, and silver, just to name a few. Why, you might ask? Money? Yes. Usefulness? Yes. Necessity? Yes. Advancement? Yes. All of the above are true. Metals add value to our lives and that is why mining is indispensable today. In a previous job setting (I have since move to another employer), I worked as a Mechanical Design Engineer with a company who created products for mining these elements from the earth. I designed the metal structures called frames on which these panels sat to separate the valuable metal from non-valuable earth. If you have ever seen the show called *Gold Rush* on cable TV, then you are familiar with the world in which my design skills got tested on a daily basis. It's what I was paid to create.

Not all metals get entertained, though. An old Pepsi cola can on the ground, rusted and dirty with age, gets overlooked by passers-by. The weathered hubcap at the local junk yard does not have a waiting list of expectant users. The ancient bicycle rim with a chunk missing as well as several spokes gets passed over for the new rim that can entertain its patrons. What about the once vibrant lawn mower, mostly metal, seasoned from years of successful operation, making its way to the landfill? No eulogies necessary. Metals can handle the departure, but may not enjoy the rejection. All of these metals made prior with purpose, but now hardly catching a glimpse of an upcoming future. Poor metals! Life just is not fair to our metallic friends.

Not <u>all</u> metals are created equal. Nothing quite compares to *precious metals.* These metals bring the flash and bling to our modern world. Why is this so? That is a great question. Here is the short answer from Wikipedia. A *precious* metal is a rare, naturally occurring metallic chemical element of *high economic value.* The best-known precious metals are the *coinage* metals, gold and silver. You heard it here, first!

The coinage metals get our attention in a <u>big</u> way. Gold and silver matter to us! They have high economic value. Our nation's currency system was founded on what could be backed by equivalent amounts of gold and silver. It was security for loans. To back a deposit with gold and silver brought comfort and confidence to the person who put money in a bank years ago. Yes, even today, over 200 plus years later, gold and silver remain as precious metals to our economy, desired greatly by all.

Funny, is it not, that God equates you and me to *gold* and *silver* all throughout the Scriptures. In the fore-knowledge of God, He knew our world system would understand the value of gold and silver and place such a high regard on its worth. In this same manner of thinking, Our Heavenly Father, describes His children in like manner. People are compared to gold and silver in the Holy Bible.

Yet, in Heaven, God's dwelling place, the Bible states that the street _is_ made of gold. What? That can't be right. God paves His Kingdom's road with pure gold. What we value so highly in our world's economy, God makes a street out of it in His Kingdom. Wow! Have we got this all messed up, today?

Let's examine the notion that God, Your Heavenly Father, would liken you and me to a precious metal. Not just any precious metal, but the coinage metals: _gold and silver._ In the book of Job, Job is put through a series of difficult tests. This _HOLY_ experiment is played out before the readers as God and the arch enemy of man, Satan, dialogue about Job's love and loyalty to God. Satan is convinced that Job is only committed to God for the benefits and his heart is connected only to the extent that he is blessed by God. God believes otherwise and allows Satan to strip Job of his earthly blessings: children, animals, farm, etc. This discourse is found in Job 1:8 – 12 (HCSB),

[8] Then the LORD said to Satan, "Have you considered My servant Job? No one else on earth is like him, a man of perfect integrity, who fears God and turns away from evil." [9] Satan answered the LORD, "Does Job fear God for nothing? [10] Haven't You placed a hedge around him, his household, and everything he owns? You have blessed the work of his hands, and his possessions have increased in the land. [11] But stretch out Your hand and strike everything he owns, and he will surely curse You to Your face." [12] "Very well," the LORD told Satan, "everything he owns is in your power. _However, you must not lay a hand on Job himself._" So, Satan left the LORD's presence.

In this _King of the Ring_ battle, Satan sets out to prove that Job is only a man of God because God has showered him with favor and blessing on his life. That question still requires immense thought today. What about you? Do you only pursue God for his hand's release or do you pursue the heart of God out of reverence and awe? Is God even on your radar for a relationship, at all? Be honest. This is _not_ a question of condemnation, rather a question of thought. Does

God get any portion of your attention each day? Just something to consider. Our buddy, Job, put God at the head of his life and teaches us a great lesson about priorities. Job shows his true bond as he learns about his changing life as found in Job 1: 13 – 22,

[13] One day when Job's sons and daughters were eating and drinking wine in their oldest brother's house, [14] a messenger came to Job and reported: "While the oxen were plowing and the donkeys grazing nearby, [15] the Sabeans swooped down and took them away. They struck down the servants with the sword, and I alone have escaped to tell you!" [16] He was still speaking when another messenger came and reported: "A lightning storm struck from heaven. It burned up the sheep and the servants and devoured them, and I alone have escaped to tell you!" [17] That messenger was still speaking when yet another came and reported: "The Chaldeans formed three bands, made a raid on the camels, and took them away. They struck down the servants with the sword, and I alone have escaped to tell you!" [18] He was still speaking when another messenger came and reported: "Your sons and daughters were eating and drinking wine in their oldest brother's house. [19] Suddenly a powerful wind swept in from the desert and struck the four corners of the house. It collapsed on the young people so that they died, and I alone have escaped to tell you!" [20] Then Job stood up, tore his robe, and shaved his head. He fell to the ground and *worshiped*, [21] saying: *Naked I came from my mother's womb, and naked I will leave this life. The LORD gives, and the LORD takes away. Praise the name of Yahweh.* [22] *Throughout all this, Job did not sin or blame God for anything.*

Job responds with flying colors in round one and states his famous line from the Word of God, *"The LORD gives, and the LORD takes away. Praise the name of Yahweh."* Our hats are off to Job in this epic story of stories. Job loses it all in a matter of minutes and his dependence on God never wavers. In fact, he inspires us <u>all</u> today to check our own hearts toward God. Job models for us, in a very tangible way, that life is about seeking God and His Righteousness (Matthew 6:33) above all else. Even in pain and powerlessness, Job presents his life in relationship to his Heavenly Father. *We should live in like manner!*

However, Satan is <u>not</u> finished with his attempts to discredit Job and show God a thing or two. Next, Satan states the final measure of Job's devotion, "Strike Job's health" and Job will defect from God's Camp. The round two battle heats up as found in Job 2:3-10

³ Then the LORD said to Satan, "Have you considered My servant Job? No one else on earth is like him, a man of perfect integrity, who fears God and turns away from evil. He still retains his integrity, even though you incited Me against him, *to destroy him without just cause.*" ⁴ *"Skin for skin!"* Satan answered the LORD. "A man will give up everything he owns in exchange for his life. ⁵ But stretch out Your hand and strike his flesh and bones, and he will surely curse You to Your face." ⁶ "Very well," the LORD told Satan, "he is in your power; *only spare his life.*" ⁷ So Satan left the LORD's presence and infected Job with terrible boils from the sole of his foot to the top of his head. ⁸ Then Job took a piece of broken pottery to scrape himself while he sat among the ashes. ⁹ His wife said to him, "Do you still retain your integrity? *Curse God and die!*" ¹⁰ "You speak as a foolish woman speaks," he told her. *"Should we accept only good from God and not adversity?" Throughout all this Job did not sin in what he said.*

WOW! Job's faith rocks! What about you? Do you see your life through these two lenses? *Wealth and health* <u>are</u> God's to portion as HE wishes. Yet, it does not make it any less difficult to navigate when we lose one or both as Job did early in his life. It is in this context that Job speaks of God in the following fashion, "But He knows the way I take; When He (God) has <u>tried</u> me, I *shall* come forth <u>as</u> gold. Job 23:10 (NASB). Job settled once and for <u>all</u> that a man or woman can love God simply out of a deep devotion and conviction. Job illustrates to all of us the truth of the "Rugged Terrain of Reality" that one's gap of expectations and one's unfolding reality can be vastly different, but it can _still_ cause us to grow, develop, and mature, in spite of life's challenges and obstacles.

Job believed that his testing would _refine_, rather than _define_, him and cause his life to become _more_ in every way. He states in a bold and confident fashion, "I shall come forth as gold" after this testing is over. I find his determination to be infectious. Notice, Job did not say, "It would be nice if I come forth as gold or in the end, gold outcomes would be my desire." _NO, Job emphatically sets the record and declares his eventual prognosis._ He is _not_ going to accept defeat, even when life is punching away. Job gets a drink of some Holy Spirit juice and perseveres in his battle. _You have the same potential._

In the end, Job is resolute in his love _for_ God, his belief _in_ God, and His loyalty _to_ God. God remains the center of his life and Job continues to turn his eyes to the One who will see him through. Becoming as gold is _never_ an easy endeavor. God has a way of removing the impurities (self-centeredness, self-promoting agendas and self-exalting exploits) so that the gold is of _purest_ account. Job passed the test. You can too!

There is one key thing I don't want you to overlook in this story line with Job. It caught my attention as I wrote this book. Notice that Satan has a master plan which, by the way, can _only_ be carried out with God's willingness and approval. Did you catch God's permission? "Very Well" was uttered in both rounds of this cosmic battle. Also, note the extent to which Satan could act. There _was_ a boundary limit or a stopping point to Satan's tactics and offense. Don't overlook this crucial truth of Job's account. Satan was _not_ given a blank check of destruction over Job's life. God was in _complete_ control and had ultimate _authority_ in this Heavenly tug-o-war. Satan is _no_ match for God! Remember, he is a created being who directed a revolt in Heaven and was cast down to earth. He is not God's equal in a dark suit because he has never been God's opposite. He is _limited_ in his purposes as allowed by God. Please allow that to sink into your mind and heart. It will serve you well in times of adversity.

Guess What? Your struggles while tiresome and non-stop, have boundaries, limits or stopping points, too. God is permitting or allowing difficult days to enter your world. Don't get offended or angry at God. What if a Heavenly dialogue is occurring over your life as well? What if God is giving Satan permission to crank up the difficulties in your life for divine outcomes. God is still in pursuit of lives of purity, devotion, and commitment. Sometimes, it takes the pressures of life to break us free from the allurements of today's society. Jesus told this very thing to Peter as found in Luke 22:31-32 (NIV),

31 "Simon, Simon, Satan has <u>asked</u> to sift *all of you* as wheat. 32 But I have prayed for you, Simon, that your faith may not fail. And when you have turned back, strengthen your brothers."

Jesus shocked the Disciples with this Upper Room chat. No one could have foreseen this testing dialogue coming, especially not Peter. Yet, in the willingness of God to create hearts of loyalty and purity, life will have a way of pushing your buttons as it were. Passing such tests, as Job illustrates, are *keys* to understanding why such Rugged Realities exist. Rugged Terrains make for successful climbers and God wants you to reach the Summit.

In a second installment, the Word of God decrees, "For you, O God, *tested* us; you refined us <u>like</u> silver." *Psalms 66:10 (NIV)*. Refine is a word reserved for selective conversations. You just don't throw that word around at many dinner parties, today. At least, I have not. Why? It only has certain meaningful applications, one being Biblical. To refine is at the heart of metallurgical engineering. It is taking metal and turning up the heat and then cooling it down, to change its metallic properties and chemistry. It is *RAW* engineering at is best.

No one wants to work at a refinery. Who would? Extremely hot, dusty, tiresome, and constant. Refineries exist today in certain parts of the world for a specific purpose. They create economic value through the means of molten change. Gold and silver come into refineries in nugget form. Rough, crude, ugly, and ignorable. Microscopic grains of value coexisting within creation's soil. These nuggets are full of earth's deposits mixed in with remnants of future currency. To the naked eye, they are unimpressive and overlooked, at least for now.

Therein lies the dilemma, gold and silver are only useful (and valuable for that matter) when the impurities are removed. No one ever wore a wedding band with dust particles as part of its package. No, my friend, gold and silver have to be pure before they become property of any end user. High school and college class rings are made of 10K, 18K, or 24K gold. The higher the number signifies more value and worth and it costs more to create and purchase as you may have experienced. I sure have.

Gold and silver *need* heat to create value and lots of it. That is why refineries are hot places. They have to be to create the effect. Gold and silver withstand change until the heat is scorching and it has no choice but to yield. The hotter the better as they say at the refinery. Why? Impurities surface when the heat is on. The Bible refers to these impurities as dross as found in Proverbs 25:4, "Remove the dross from the silver, and a silversmith can produce a vessel." That is not a household word today. Have you ever heard of such a word? Dross affects the worth of the material. It sabotages the material's destiny. Therefore, heat is applied to create change.

Refinery workers are skilled at creating a dross party. This has to be removed to create purity of substance. Have you ever wondered, "What is the ideal temperature to allow the dross to surface to the top of the molten metal?" Great Question! Research shows that smelters look for their reflections in the molten material when the heat reaches its ideal temperature. In effect, the hot material becomes as a mirror <u>and</u> the smelter can see his reflection in the gold or silver. Pretty cool stuff as I see it.

What a parallel to your real-life dynamics. The material (gold and sliver) undergoes change (heat) and the smelter (God) can see His reflection in the pure metal. WOW! That is amazing. Are you beginning to see that God is *not* random in ordering or allowing our lives to unfold as they do? No, He is permitting life to *create* pure metals called gold and silver and we are benefited in the end. No one ever liked heat, but heat produces purity and usefulness. *Welcome the smelter's touch.*

One final place for our time together, the Holy Bible makes it known once again, "³ He will sit as a refiner and purifier of silver; he will purify the Levites and *refine* them like gold and silver. Then the Lord will have men (and woman, too) who will bring offerings in righteousness, ⁴ and the offerings of Judah and Jerusalem will be acceptable to the Lord, as in days gone by, as in former years. *Malachi 3:3-4 (NIV)*. In this series of verses, the heart of God is revealed, *Righteousness.* God seeks to create opportunities in our lives for righteousness (right living) to develop. Another complementary word (and Biblical) is called holiness. Righteousness and holiness are at the core of Christ-centered living. Yet, in our fallen state, we don't always make these two targets our aim. However, in the providence of God, adversity, trials, pressures, and struggles allow our impurities to surface. In times like these, God brings to the forefront of our lives the dross that needs to be removed. Our lives are better for it. God's imprint is evident on our lives when righteousness and holiness prevail. It is worth it to see the by-product of being tried, tested, refined, and purified. Can you say the same? It won't happen at first, though!

Take a few minutes as we close this chapter to ask God what areas of your life have impurities or dross. Maybe, its an attitude of condemnation toward others? Could it be a secret habit or sin that you entertain when no one else is watching? Are you struggling with lust of the heart toward the opposite sex or even the same sex for that matter? Do you have filthy language pouring out of your mouth at work, at home, with your friends, or at the golf course? Are you defined as a negative thinking individual? Do you always see the glass as half empty and bemoaning life's obstacles as a victim of your environment? Is pride your sin of choice as you feel smug about your self-made accomplishment and material gains? Finally, do you celebrate laziness as a virtue to wear, rather than a sin to slay? Do you sit back waiting on others to wait on you and believe you are entitled to such service? This list could go on and on and you would get my point. God wants to create righteousness and holiness in your life. Precious metals <u>need</u> heat and *you* are precious to God. He will give the "Very Well" permission to bolster change in your life at any cost. Tried, tested, refined, and purified are *worth* it all. Don't shun these words as *curse* words and get angry with God, the devil, or life as they visit your home. Yield to them and watch the way your life increases with purpose, power, and peace. Gold and silver still turn heads, today. Follow Job's declaration, ""But He knows the way I take; When He (God) has *tried* me, I *shall* come forth <u>as</u> gold. *Job 23:10 (NASB). That my friend is purposeful living.*

It's Your Move!

I. Precious Metals. You are precious to God. Do you believe this truth? _____.

2. What would it take for you to let this truth sink into your soul? _____.

3. The Heat is on! What areas of your life are heating up?

   a._____.

   b. _____.

   c._____.

4. In what ways to you relate to Job? a. _____

   b. _____ c. _____.

5. Have you surrendered your heart to God? Why or why not? _____.

6. Would you like to know God, personally? Turn to the last chapter about "Inviting Jesus Christ into your heart."

10

The Fire Factor

Have you ever been camping? I have. If you have, then you would know that the highlight of the trip is when the camp fire gets started in the evenings. Sure, it is intended to keep the mosquitos away, but more than that it is the time when people gather together to tell stories, laugh at life, roast marshmallows, and sing songs. (every campfire almost creates guitar players out of nowhere. You can't have a REAL campfire without someone bringing out the guitar.) In any event, we love the way camp fires make us feel. We build special memories from our mixing with others and the uncertainties of daily living seem to slip away while we are celebrating the beauty of our shared adventure called *Life*.

What about in your home? Do you have a fireplace? Do you ever sit and watch the fire roar and crackle? I do. Do you enjoy the warmth it brings? (not the greatest heat source, but surely the most enjoyable). The beauty of a fire is what makes for a dreamy nightfall among couples and the environment is set for a romantic evening.

Yes, a fire has a way of setting the mood and creating outcomes that ALL couples are zealous to achieve. Whether a camp fire or a fire in your fireplace, the thrill of the fire is alluring and captivating. Fire has a purpose!

God uses fire, too, in an entirely different manner, but it is also *captivating* and has a *purpose*. Let's examine God's agenda for fire as noted in the following statement below:

FIRE is the vehicle by which God begins to ORIENT your life from a SELF–CENTERED and SELF-DIRECTED pursuit to a God-Honoring and God-Exalting PASSION and PURPOSE for living.

Now, before you begin to think I am getting a little too preachy and pushy with that statement, I want you to hit the pause button. *You have the freedom at all times, while reading this book, to act as you so choose.* You can decide what to do with any part of this book's content and how it impacts and affects your life. I am simply sharing from my observations of over 25 plus years of studying people's circumstances and dynamics. In addition, I am adding in my own life experiences into this recipe. I know of what I am speaking and I don't want you to feel pressured in any way. Yes, God wants to create a pathway for blessing, joy, and peace in your life. I believe that to always be *true*. However, we (or "you" if you want to make it personal) must first acknowledge and admit that we are self-centered and self-directed in our own agendas for life. We all have self-interests and often leave God *completely* out of a lot of it. *If we were totally truthful, the majority of our hardships in life occur from poor decisions, impulsive actions, and good old-fashioned pride.* We must be authentic here! Now is not the time to candy-coat our true identities. Notice, I didn't say all the time because we have all experienced the effects of another's actions and had to pick up the pieces of our broken lives. You didn't ask to be abused. You didn't ask to get rejected. You didn't ask to experience a divorce. You didn't ask to be humiliated. You didn't want to be let go from your current job.

You didn't ask to be broken by life's unknowns. I totally understand your sentiments and would agree that you've hit some walls in your daily agenda. However, let's look at life, including your life, from a little higher vantage point.

If I could share a bit of my heart with you as I write this chapter. The previous chapter's content flowed quite easy for me, but this chapter has not been that way. Please let me explain. There were days I would get up early to write this chapter, only to stop after a few lines of writing. To be honest, this was quite frustrating to this new "author" because I had an internal deadline that I want to complete this book by. *However, God put the brakes on each time and I knew it.* There was something *bigger* happening and I had to be open to God moving in me so I could transfer it to you.

Why is this chapter taking time I would ask myself? I believe it's because this chapter holds such significance in your life in God's Economy. Additionally, it is a *Turning Point* for this book as a whole. It holds in its power a pivotal moment for you as the reader. Together, we are now at a familiar crossroads. This intersection haunts many a reader and produces the "I'm in" or "I'm out" for Ideal (and Reality) living. There are *only* two options from this point forward (at least as I see it, so please continue to read on). *There is no half-hearted dancing in the rain from this point forward.* I am recognizing this now after several months of trying to finish this chapter. It is not just about rushing some words on a page to complete a chapter called *The Fire Factor.* No, God wants to use this chapter to change your life and *change your view of God* in difficult times and seasons of life.

As I write, I am aware of God's desire to bring your life to a fuller and richer place, *a place of growth, maturity, and grace.* Nevertheless, I am also aware of the vehicle that God uses to generate this kind of life, F.I.R.E. I wish for everyone's sake that there were an easier method or route. As of yet, *Fire* still proves to produce the most beneficial, albeit painful results. Let me try to illustrate this point in a tangible way.

In my personal time with God during the last few months, I have been reading about the life of Joseph. The Dreamer, as he is called, in the book of Genesis, Chapters 37 – 50. I would suggest you read these impactful chapters as they are filled with excitement, intrigue and adventure. For me, I have read and re-read these chapters over and over again in pursuit of nuggets of life-changing gold.

This season of learning about Joseph's life is the *precise* reason this chapter has been delayed. What my spirit is learning needs to be applied to this chapter. Because I don't assume you know about this incredible person named Joseph, I will share parts of his life's journey as it applies to this chapter.

Let's begin with this understanding about God's agenda for your life. *The Fire Factor is personal for everyone.* It is individual in its makeup and intent. No copier story lines or scripts here in life's dress rehearsal. No two approaches or outcomes, from God's directive, are identical. You see God knows you better than you know yourself and He is fully aware of the *Fire* that gets *your* attention. He <u>really</u> does. You have to give Him that! However, with complete love and consideration for your life, He wants to move you to higher ground and it takes a test and trial to create a willing participant, and sometimes not so willing I might add. As my former Pastor, Ron Carpenter of Redemption Church in San Jose, CA often says, "God has not lost a battle, yet". Therefore, yielding to the wake of God's purpose brings the liberating fruit of change in your life. But, it can sometimes hurt too.

I can assure you that God knows what He is doing. In fact, the Bible declares that He knows your life from the end to the beginning as found in Isaiah 46:10 (NIV), "I make known the end from the beginning, from ancient times, what is still to come. I say, 'My purpose will stand, and I will do all that I please." Yes, God is in complete control of your life and has recorded your days in eloquent fashion as echoed by David as recorded in Psalms 139:13 – 16 (CEB), "You are the one who created my innermost parts; you knit me together while I was still in my mother's womb. [14] I give thanks to you that I was marvelously set apart. Your works are wonderful—I know that very well. [15] My bones weren't hidden from you when I was being put together in a secret place, when I was being woven together in the deep parts of the earth. [16] Your eyes saw my embryo, and on your scroll every day was written that was being formed for me, before any one of them had yet happened." Did *you* catch that? God *knows* you, personally. You are hand-crafted by the mighty hand of God, a Masterpiece in the making. *And*, you matter to God! *Your life has His attention!*

Here is the reality as I see it. We march forward in life with our goals, to-do lists, and agendas, giving little consideration of how God would fit into our lives. Interestingly enough though, God brings about change in an unusual way. This leads us to the next nugget of gold as stated below:

Trials are __NECESSARY__ because they give __YOU__ an __OPPORTUNITY__ to see __INSIDE YOURSELF__, and to take a __LOOK__ at the "__REAL YOU__" – The __YOU__ that only GOD sees. THEN, GOD goes On a Mission with YOU for YOUR __REFINEMENT__.

I have a great friend who was a corporate chaplain. In fact, he was our company chaplain at my mining engineering job. My dear friend, Gene Pace, led our weekly Bible study called "Keeping Pace...Where Life and Faith Cross". I often heard him proclaim this very thought. He would say, "Reputation is who others think you are, but character is who your *really* are." What was he saying here? Our chaplain was implying that you have a public you and a private you. However, God wants those two worlds to merge into one you.

Let's face it for what it is. Difficult circumstances bring out the *best* or *worst* in us. When you squeeze an orange, you get orange juice. However, when we get squeezed by life, we often get surprised by what surfaces. Nevertheless, God is not surprised. He sees the *real* you and cares enough to initiate change to occur. If God knows your life from the end to the beginning, He is working to create opportunities to bring about change in your world and surgically remove the cancerous attitudes, destructive habits, negative thinking, and selfish pursuits from your life, just to name a few. *It has God's attention when you live outside of His best for your life.*

Notice, I said that "Trials are necessary". I can sense a bit of pushback from you as I pushed back also for far too many years. No one likes a trial and I certainly would agree. However, human nature will dance around issues for years, never evaluating the destruction they are causing in relationships, purpose, peace, and joy. It is easier to accept your flaws and simply go on with life as normal. *Yet, God is not about to bend on this. Why? Because God wants to introduce "you" to yourself so you can begin removing the poison inside your heart.* Situations bring out the <u>real</u> you, the *you* that only God sees! God cares enough to say, "If you don't deal with issues today when they are small and manageable, then down the road, they will capsize the ship of your life and harm other individuals in the process. Wrong behavior <u>never</u> occurs in a vacuum, hurting only the singular party. No, wrong behavior (or sin as the Bible calls it) creates explosions in which many are wounded and impacted.

Looking inside ourselves, as God sees us, is often scary and intimidating. Why? The truthful answer is that everyone has skeletons in his or her closet. You know it, others know it, and most of all, God knows it. Up till now, those toxic areas of your life, if left unattended and ignored, will sabotage your future and make your present tremendously burdensome. God sees the carnage of your life's habits, hurts, and hang-ups. With a caring and loving heart, your Heavenly Father sets out to craft opportunities for those areas to surface and be dealt with and finally removed. It is equivalent to a wound that is *never* adequately cleaned can by no means properly be healed. It is simple to say, but particularly complex to do.

Nevertheless, God knows you *intimately* and will *uncompromisingly* pursue those injurious heart conditions and graciously move them to exposure and extraction from your life. *Notice, I didn't say God leaves you to figure out how to improve your life alone.* Absolutely not! God partners with you in the same way a loving father would tend to a needy son or daughter to provide healing, help, hope, and encouragement. That is a wonderful thought if you stop to think about it.

The Fire Factor hit the life of Joseph in an *enormous* way. It is fascinating to read his account in the Bible. I will share some details of Joseph's struggles and declare how it relates to you and me. Let's unpack the heart of God to bring Joseph to a place of humility, maturity, conviction, determination, purpose, and leadership.

Joseph was a boastful kid with a look-at-me attitude. His brothers knew that he was his daddy's favorite and the royal coat only served to make that overtly known as noted in Genesis 37:1-4 (CEB), "Jacob lived in the land of Canaan where his father was an immigrant. ² This is the account of Jacob's descendants. Joseph was 17-years-old and tended the flock with his brothers. While he was helping the sons of Bilhah and Zilpah, his father's wives, Joseph <u>told</u> their father unflattering things about them. *³ Now Israel loved Joseph more than any of his other sons because he was born when Jacob was old. Jacob had made for him a long robe.* ⁴ When his brothers saw that their father loved him more than any of his brothers, *they hated him* and couldn't even talk nicely to him."

Is it any wonder that the Bible declares that "They hated him"? Surely, that is strong language for a Biblical family. Still, it was quite evident that Joseph's brothers felt chided by him. Take note that Jacob was using Joseph to be a snitch regarding his brother's behavior and their ability to tend the family sheep. Joseph was often sent out to spy on the brother's activity and Jacob was informed of any misdealing Joseph saw. If that was *not* enough, the famous coat of many colors (as one translation puts it) was the proverbial straw that broke the camel's back as the brothers witnessed the obvious favoritism toward

Joseph. As you can see, we have a dysfunctional family right here in the Bible for all to read. *There is hope for us all.*

To add insult to injury, Joseph had a series of two dreams regarding his future and the family heritage. Now keep in mind, the brothers <u>already</u> hated this cocky youngster. Here is how the story line unfolds as found in Genesis 37: 5-11 (CEB), *"⁵ Joseph had a dream and told it to his brothers, which made them hate him even more.* ⁶ He said to them, "Listen to this dream I had. ⁷ When we were binding stalks of grain in the field, my stalk got up and stood upright, while your stalks gathered around it and *bowed down to my stalk."* ⁸ His brothers said to him, "Will you really be our king and rule over us?" So, they hated him *even more* because of the dreams he told them. ⁹ Then Joseph had <u>another</u> dream and described it to his brothers: "I've just dreamed again, and this time the sun and the moon and eleven stars were *bowing down to me."* ¹⁰ When he described it to his father and brothers, his father scolded him and said to him, "What kind of dreams have you dreamed? Am I and your mother and your brothers supposed to come and bow down to the ground in front of you?" ¹¹ His brothers were jealous of him, but his father took careful note of the matter."

This is undoubtedly a script for a modern reality show. Just imagine that you have a sibling and he or she comes up to you one morning and says, "Guess what? I had a dream, two times actually, in which the whole family was bowing to me, including Mom and Dad!" I may be stretching my holy imagination a bit, but your siblings would say you have been "smoking a few left-handed roll-your-owns". The nerve of Joseph to share such an in-your-face declaration with his brothers who already hated him. *Why would Joseph do such an outlandish thing?* That is a good question! Joseph had a lot to learn in the realm of humility, honor, and building healthy, long-standing relationships. Joseph stubbed his toe with his brothers and their treatment of him was over the top.

Joseph finds himself in a pickle as his dad, Israel, once again sends him to inquire of the brothers' activity while tending the family flock. In the distance, the brothers see the *Golden Boy* and plot to kill him as stated in Genesis 37:18 – 20 (CEB), "[18] They saw Joseph in the distance before he got close to them, and *they plotted to kill him*. [19] The brothers said to each other, "Here comes the big dreamer. [20] Come on now, let's kill him and throw him into one of the cisterns, and we'll say a wild animal devoured him. Then we will see what becomes of his dreams!"". *You heard that correctly. They were going to murder him!*

The emotions had come to a boiling point and they, the ruthless brothers, determined to end the Dreamer's life. The eldest brother, Reuben, came to Joseph's defense and suggested placing the boy in a cistern, thinking he would come back later to rescue him. The resentful crew agreed to honor Reuben's appeal and preserve the lad's life. However, in an attempt to make a little money, they agreed to sell him as a common slave to a band of traders, heading for Egypt. At this time, we will pause the story and pick it back up in Chapter 11 to learn about Joseph's fate.

Lets' take a minute and bring this chapter home to real life. Even if you are *not* a Bible reader or wonder if the Bible is true and can be trusted, take this story for what it is. Joseph is about to experience the *Fire* of his life. He will begin to see *huge* changes coming to his world in a profound way. While God didn't cause it, He permitted it to happen. And, it is for Joseph's good as it will turn out!

Nonetheless, I sometimes wonder if we (or you) see the *big* picture when trials, troubles, test, or tragedies come our (your) way. For emphasis, let me put these two nuggets of gold next to each other one more time to internalize:

FIRE is the vehicle by which God begins to ORIENT your life from a SELF–CENTERED and SELF-DIRECTED quest to a God-Honoring and God-Exalting PASSION and PURPOSE for living.

Trials are __NECESSARY__ because they give __YOU__ an __OPPORTUNITY__ to see __INSIDE YOURSELF__, and to take a __LOOK__ at the "__REAL YOU__" — The __YOU__ that only GOD sees. THEN, GOD goes On a Mission with YOU for YOUR __REFINEMENT__. (italics added)

My Dear Friend,

If I had a chance to sit with you one-on-one, I would ask you a deep and riveting question. Not to make you feel uncomfortable, or criticize, but rather to help point you in a healthier and more joyful direction. My question simply stated is this,

"What area or areas of your life are leaving you feeling less than abundant, purposeful, empowering, or victorious?"

When I ask such a question, you don't have to think long for an answer to surface. Why? We __all__ have our hot button areas that strike chords of frustration, anger, confusion, or tears. *That is nothing to be ashamed of.* Quite the contrary! *Every life is unique and every face tells a different story.* The ingredients of each person's dynamic make *every* life a masterpiece, nevertheless, at the same time, creates hurdles to jump and mountains to move. What is it for you? Write them in the margin beside this text. Go ahead! Put it on paper. Get it out in the open, at least for yourself, to acknowledge. God already knows and it is time for you to confess and agree with God about it.

The beauty of this chapter is that while *many* see God as a Heavenly Killjoy or a Holy Traffic Cop, eager to write Biblical citations, God is loving, patient, concerned, and available. He seeks your *best* and wants to walk (on a mission) with you through the tough changes ahead. He is *not* disengaged or disinterested in your daily battles, weaknesses, or losses in life. *Just the opposite, my Dear Friend!*

At this point, take a minute to put the book down. Yes, that's right. Put the book down for a moment and *step outside*, if you can.

Marvin Robert Wohlhueter, Th.D.

Stop and look at what is around you. What do you see?

For in every season, the hand of God is evident. In the winter months, no two snow flakes are exactly a like, from Buffalo to Colorado. In the spring time, the up-and-coming trees are brimming with anticipation for new life and buds to appear. In the rays of summer, the flowers are pregnant with beauty, from every color of the rainbow. In the fall, it is the wonder of transitioning leaves, altering from green to orange, yellow, red, and burgundy. Have you seen these proofs of God's care and concern for His Creation? What about your life? Are there proofs of His care and concern for you? This same God sees you as an image bearer, His image, for that matter! *You have to grasp that!*

You are important to God. Your life has always had His attention. Any portion, <u>less</u> than His best, will have a *Fire* potential for change. Now, don't run from it. Embrace it. Don't see it as a blemish. See it as an opportunity for blessing. Don't *fear* it. Rather, *face* it. God's not picking on you. No, He is passionate about you! However, like Joseph, your life has some maturing to do. We all do! That is the wonder (and burden, at times) of life! We have the potential to make our lives healthier, fuller, and more purposeful. To make it personal, with God by your side, the best is coming your way. Joseph is about to see God at work as *The Fire Factor* comes. So, can you...In a Good way...A God way! Thank you for allowing me to share such a challenging word in this Chapter. They are not easy to swallow. I know that very well. Yet, necessary, nonetheless. Whew! Tough chapter.

Let me share a quick personal story that Lorraine and I were facing as I wrote this chapter. *Fire* stories never seem to let up and that can tend to get challenging, but trusting God is imperative to move forward with a Living hope. Lorraine had a rental house in Atlanta, Georgia. The tenants had elected to stay in the home even after the lease was up. No rent, no intention of leaving, no moral character, no fear of legal recourse. In the wake of this entitlement era, the tenants were unwilling to leave peacefully. We took them to magistrate court for an eviction. We won that day and a date was set to have them move out. Guess what? The tenants appealed the court's decision. What? You heard me right. No regard to honor *this* Judge and *his* wisdom. Now, we were heading to Superior Court. What is going on?

The notion of going to Superior Court was a little scary and extremely frustrating. Time, money, weariness, emotional angst, anger, stress, etc. These are <u>real</u> life ingredients and factors that come into play in reality living. There were days you wondered if you can handle the pressure and pain of such overwhelming circumstances. This was normal. The long and short of the story was that we had to pay over $5000 in legal fees to get them out. And, guess what? They trashed the place before leaving our rental home. What? You heard me right! We had to completely remodel the house with out-of-pocket money. Can you believe it? Sometimes, life is not fair.

I am not alone in my lament to God for the *Fire* that falls my way. However, I can't leave the heart of God out of the equation. Yes, it hurts. Yes, it is exhausting. Yes, it is unfair. Yes, it is painful. Yes, it is costly. No one would disagree with these statements. I choose to believe that <u>my</u> God is a Good God and that, while I may not like what I am going through, <u>He</u> is creating in me the purest gold that can enhance my life in the future. Don't overlook His purposes, even in your agony. Now, Let's move on to Chapter 11.

It's Your Move!

I. The Fire Factor. What does this title mean to you now that you finished the chapter? _____

_____.

2. No one likes trials! What trials are you in now? a. _____

_____ b. _____ c. _____.

3. Does God have your attention? How? _____

_____.

4. In what ways do you relate to Joseph's life? _____

_____

_____.

5. List four ways you are asking God for change in your life?

a. _____.

b. _____.

c. _____.

d. _____.

11

The Price You Pay for Purity

When we left Joseph, he was on his way to Egypt. He was sold as a common slave, by his own brothers, as noted in Genesis 37: 28, "When the Midianite merchants came by, Joseph's brothers took him out of the well, and for twenty pieces of silver they *sold him* to the Ishmaelites who took him to Egypt." (CEV). Wow! His own flesh and blood sold him for a small amount of capital. As surprising as this seems to hear or bear, Joseph had <u>no</u> value in his brother's eyes, relationally that is. Why is it that those closest to you are willing to trade you for a minimal exchange? Joseph could *not* convince his brothers to reconsider his fate. *Don't be surprised when you can't either.*

Why? Life demands that you have a price tag. While God deems you as priceless, the world is <u>not</u> as kind, nor fair with your value. The screams of your worth are all around you. Some offer you at bargain-base pricing. Many will sell you at the yard sale of opportunity if they can benefit from your misfortune. Still, others plant seeds of worthlessness in your head and you end up selling yourself for mere pennies. On the other hand, you may even _give_ yourself away at no cost to anyone. You feel used, trampled on, degraded, and often overlooked. That is such a catastrophe from God's view point, though. You see your worth and value through the wrong set of lenses. Tragically, you march on through life with a misrepresentation of what you have to _offer_ the world and God's Kingdom.

Nevertheless, God has _settled_ the issue of your value on the Cross. His One and Only Son, Jesus Christ, was the going price for your soul. Nonetheless, in life, you _must_ decide the value of your _own_ existence. While the world will _flaunt_ your commonness, God paid a high price for your uniqueness. You are a _One-of-a-Kind_ work of art. Sadly; Joseph's brothers saw no irreplaceable value in the young chap. They could not give honor to Joseph for who he was as a member of the family or a creation of Almighty God. His brothers were quick to label him as disposable and discarded him. _As a result, Joseph got sold without even a warning!_

Lest we forget, God is always at work in the lives of His Creation to bring about maturity and growth. Joseph was right where God was working. Nothing caught God by surprise, even for Joseph's untimely state of affairs. As hard as that is to process, the Bible assures us that God is working all through our lives for His Glory. And, strange as it may be, Joseph got sold a second time as outlined in Genesis 37: 36, "Meanwhile, the Midianites had sold Joseph in Egypt to a man named Potiphar, who was the king's official in charge of the palace guard." (CEV). _Joseph was now in position for Fire to start maturing and transforming him into a future Leader._

Let's pause for a moment and address the _bigger_ question at-hand. Why does God allow people to go through adverse and uncomfortable experiences, circumstances, or times of testing? Joseph would shout a hearty _Amen_ at this moment. Joseph, while a little smug and cocky, was not really bothering anyone. Why, boys will be boys, and every family has some sibling conflict. Many would exclaim that Joseph was just being a teenager. Parents, from all nations would agree, that teenagers are different people (Our Pastor, Jenetzen Franklin, said, "For 4 to 6 years, teenagers just lose their minds." Would you agree?)

While I agree with your sentiments, God had a bigger purpose for Joseph's life (and God's people as we shall learn later) and these events provided the pathway for His preparation and involvement. But, more than that, God wanted to work into Joseph's life the very same ingredients He seeks to impart to yours. *Can I give us a snapshot into God's heart for his Creation?* While He invites us to "come as we are", He loves us too much to let us stay there! Hence, God is purposeful in bringing about *Fire* to initiate movement toward changing our lives for our good and His Glory!

I can hear you say, "How does God make this happen?" That is a great question. God has a *proven* approach. Let's explore briefly God's *Method, Motive, Mission, and Mandate* for sacred change. Once we become aware of a Heavenly Father who will guide, direct, correct, and instruct us to living the *best* life possible, we can <u>accept</u> the tenets of God's agenda. Let me break it down briefly below.

God has a Method, a proven one, that has worked throughout ages past and present, and will work in the future. God (the Master Refiner) brings the *Fire* (the heat of life).

The Refiner's <u>Method</u> - Fire

"You have caused men to ride over our heads; We went <u>through</u> fire and <u>through</u> water; But You brought us out <u>to rich *fulfillment.*</u>" *Psalms 66:12 (NKJV)*

"When you pass <u>through</u> the waters, I will be with you; and when you pass <u>through</u> the rivers, they will not sweep over you. When you walk <u>through</u> the fire, you will not be burned; the flames will <u>not</u> set you ablaze. For I am the LORD, your God, the Holy One of Israel, your Savior;" Isaiah *43:2-3 (NIV)*

Notice, in both Scriptures, that God brings you <u>through</u> the *Fire. Fire is <u>never</u> meant to consume you, but rather to refine you.* Put another way, the heat of life has a way of making things flexible, yielding to the new destiny or purpose. Remember, we learned earlier that dross, from the gold and silver, surfaces as a result of applied heat. The impurities become evident and easier to remove when they make their way to the surface. Change is possible when the mind and heart begin to renew as a result of pressure, both internal and external. The once unwilling individual now begins to give in to God's maturing process and receives opportunities for spiritual growth and increasing vitality. This leads us to the next nugget of Truth.

The Refiner's <u>Motive</u> - To Purge and Purify

"Remove the dross from the silver, and out comes material for the silversmith; remove the wicked from the king's presence, and his throne will be established through righteousness." *Proverbs 25:4-5 (NIV)*

"But in a great house there are not only vessels of gold and silver, but also of wood and clay, *some for honor* and some for dishonor. Therefore, if anyone cleanses himself from the latter, he will be a *<u>vessel for honor</u>,* sanctified and useful for the Master, prepared for every good work." *2 Timothy 2:20-21 (NKJV)*

This step leads one to introspection. Looking inside is never easy or fun, yet God wants you to begin to evaluate your life in light of *His Best.* The Bible paints a picture of what right living looks like. It is not haughty, but authentic. The Bible word is called righteousness and will be discussed in more detail below. However, for now, let's examine five key areas of your life as it relates to living in a manner *attractive* to God. While there are many specifics of behavior and impact, these five areas provide a healthy backdrop for you to uncover your life dynamics and God's hope to *purge* and *purify* in your life.

1. *Character* – How does your character line up with God's ideals for right living? What would others say about your life? When no one else is looking, God sees the intents of your heart and the inner workings of your soul. Do you know who you are, deep down at your core? Character still matters, today! It's worth a look inside.

2. *Conduct* – How do your actions line up with God's yearning for right living and eternal value? Everyday, your behavior is representing you for positive or negative. You have a choice to act in a manner that is fruitful for your life and pleasing to the God who created you.

3. *Communication* – How does your speech line up with God's truth? Words are powerful! Everyone has been hurt with harsh words and its damaging effect. Conversely, everyone has been blessed with words of kindness, care, love, and hope. You can either lift people up or bring them down with words. God does not take this one lightly. Seek to bless others!

4. *Convictions* – How do your principles line up with God's standards? The foundation of your life must be built on truths that stand the test of time. When the storms of life descend, do you have the means to weather them? Your conviction is the anchor to hold you in life's sway. What do you believe in and why? You have to know this pivotal ingredient to your existence. If not, others will hand you their truths and opinions about what to hold dear to your heart and soul. Seek God to plant deep in your heart His

foundation for true living. It will serve you <u>all</u> the days of your life.

5. *Connection* — How does your ability to interact and engage with others line up with God's love for people, *all* types of people? Do you relate well with others? It is crucial to be able to flow into the lives of all categories of people. Diversity is the spice of life, as they say. People of all upbringings, including race, gender identity, ethnicity, socio-economic ranks, sexual orientation, religious beliefs, and education levels, are precious to God. Do you treat *all* as you would want to be treated? The Golden Rule is constantly in play here. Give others your best! You'll be glad you did.

Yes, my Dear Friend, God is passionate about your character, conduct, communication, convictions, and connections. He purposes each area to be a blessing to your life and not a detriment to healthy living. *In the end, the effort to purge and purify is on God's agenda.* Let me help you to break this down into bite-size morsels. On a scale from 0 to 10, with 0 being "needs work" and 10 being "doing great", write in the margin, beside each ingredient, how you are doing. Keep in mind that there is no right or wrong for this, *only awareness.* Don't beat yourself up if you are struggling in a particular area. It is only a starting point for change. Every journey begins with a "You are here" consciousness.

You must understand that God's concern is <u>progress</u>, not <u>pace</u> for change. This should free you up to enjoy the journey of transformation. I even will add that it may include two steps forward, three steps back. Never give up! Keep moving toward the 10, regardless how life strives to keep you moving backwards. Check back in one month, three months, six months, and one year. Write the new scale down. Are you moving toward God's best for your life in these five *huge* areas? God will walk with you. He always does! I know what you may be thinking, "Why is God so focused on right living?" Great question! That leads us to the Refiner's Mission.

The Refiner's Mission - Your Righteousness

"Then the LORD will have men who will bring offerings in righteousness, Malachi 3:3b (NIV)

As for me, I will see Your face in righteousness; I shall be satisfied when I awake in Your likeness. Psalms 17:15 (NKJV)

"I put on righteousness as my clothing;" Job 29:14 (NIV)

Every great enterprise, or organization needs a mission statement, a guiding star, a purpose for being. God is no different. He has a Mission for your life, in a word, Righteousness. I know that's a big word and kind of churchy feeling, but let me bring it down to every day living. To help create some low hanging fruit understanding, I went to the synonyms in this Word program for righteousness. What I found might shed some light on the mantra of God's Mission. The synonyms that jumped out at me were virtue, decency, uprightness, and blamelessness.

God is seeking to create in you, at the core of your being, a desire for upright and virtuous living. This mantra is not merely a behavioral workshop mentality, but a gut-level core change into God-like-ness. Now before you push back or resist alterations, what I am describing is an inner root that will naturally produce like-in-kind fruit. In other words, God wants to begin with the seed or heart of a thing, and the effects will produce the sought-after outcomes. What comes to your mind when you think of the words: righteousness or holiness? Mother Teresa? Billy Graham? Martin Luther King, or Princess Diana? While these were certainly great people, their first step to right living is the same as yours.

God's Mission is the same for every human being! The challenge is the level of acceptance and implementation for each life. Yes, we tend to see and evaluate the outcomes of the Mother Teresa's or the Billy Graham's, but the process of tweaking, adjusting, correcting, or transforming a life is little-by-little as God brings the *Fire* and creates opportunity for the dross to surface as noted earlier. In the end, your life creates a <u>reflection</u> of your Heavenly Father that touches those around you. In effect, you become God's spokesman or spokeswoman. These leads us to the final directive: Be My Witness!

The Refiner's <u>Mandate</u> ~ Be a Witness for God

"Soak me in your laundry and I'll come out clean, scrub me and I'll have a snow-white life. Tune me in to foot-tapping songs, set these once-broken bones to dancing. Don't look too close for blemishes, give me a clean bill of health. God, make a fresh start in me, shape a Genesis week from the chaos of my life. Don't throw me out with the trash, or fail to breathe holiness in me. Bring me back from gray exile, put a fresh wind in my sails! *Give me a job teaching rebels your ways so the lost can find their way home." Psalms 51:7-13 (MSG)*

These verses sound refreshing and down-to-earth. Yes, 24/7/365, year-after-year kind of wording. Why? Because we all can relate to having a new song placed into our hearts and a clean bill of health pronounced over our lives. However, the context for these verses might shock you if you are not familiar with King David. The Bible described David as a "Man after God's Own Heart". Nonetheless, David had his own brand of human dysfunction. The above verses come after a year of trying to cover up an affair with Bathsheba, having her husband, Uriah, purposely killed in battle so he (David) can take her as his own wife (she was now pregnant with his child), the child eventually dies, and Nathan, the man of God, confronts David to finally come clean about his behavior. David, deep with remorse and conviction, finally cries out to God for forgiveness and asks for a new start with his Heavenly Father. God hears David's heart-felt plea.

He recognizes the grace of God and states that which would come naturally as a result of his guilt and shame burden being lifted, *"Give me a job teaching rebels your ways so the lost can find their way home."* God, like King David, is inviting you and me to help individuals find their way home. This has always been God's heart for His Creation. Home is where the heart resides and equally, home is where peace lives. My Dear Friend, *the Essence of Life is a life full of Peace.* Hence, God's Method, Motive, Mission, and Mandate are centered around bringing individuals, the world over, to a *life of peace that surpasses human understanding.* Only God can deliver that! *Only God cares and loves you enough to see that you get it!*

Remember Joseph? What has he been doing since we last talked about him? Things went from bad, to worse, to out-and-out crazy. Joseph was sold to Potiphar as noted previously. However, Potiphar's wife apparently had needs not being met by the man of the house. She pursued Joseph to enjoy her femininity and womanly fruits as noted in Genesis 39:6-10, "[6-7] Joseph was a strikingly handsome man. As time went on, his master's wife became infatuated with Joseph and one day said, "Sleep with me." [8-9] He wouldn't do it. He said to his master's wife, "Look, with me here, my master doesn't give a second thought to anything that goes on here—he's put me in charge of everything he owns. He treats me as an equal. The only thing he hasn't turned over to me is you. You're his wife, after all! How could I violate his trust and sin against God?" [10] She pestered him day after day after day, but he stood his ground. He refused to go to bed with her." (MSG)

What's wrong with a little cuddling among friends was the thought on Potiphar's wife's mind. She was determined to seduce the young man and make him one of her lunchtime meals. However, Joseph refused to honor her demands. In most circles, this would have been notable and everyone would clap for Joseph's moral stand. Yet, his refusal of his boss' wife made her all the more resolute to watch the Hebrew boy surrender to her sexual wishes. All was not well at Boomtown! Potiphar's wife was persistent as noted in Genesis 39:11-15, "[11-15] On one of these days he came to the house to do his work and none of the household servants happened to be there. She grabbed him by his cloak, saying, "Sleep with me!" He left his coat in her hand and ran out of the house. When she realized that he had left his coat in her hand and run outside, she called to her house servants: "Look—this Hebrew shows up and before you know it he's trying to seduce us. He tried to make love to me but I yelled as loud as I could. With all my yelling and screaming, he left his coat beside me here and ran outside." (MSG)

The scene has now been set for a mock rape charge and Potiphar's wife is unwavering to frame Joseph. In a "He said, she said" battle with Potiphar, Joseph is doomed. The wife of the top dog will always prevail over the servant. Nothing that Joseph said to convince Potiphar of his innocence would have mattered at this point. Yes, once again, Joseph's world is spiraling out of control as Potiphar's' wife delivers the knock-out punch as noted in Genesis 39:19-23, "[19-23] When his master heard his wife's story, telling him, "These are the things your slave did to me," he was furious. Joseph's master took him and threw him into the jail where the king's prisoners were locked up. *But there in jail GOD was still with Joseph:* He reached out in kindness to him; he put him on good terms with the head jailer. The head jailer put Joseph in charge of all the prisoners—*he ended up managing the whole operation.* The head jailer gave Joseph free rein, never even checked on him, because GOD was with him; *whatever he did GOD made sure it worked out for the best."* (MSG)

Are you logging the offenses against Joseph thus far in his young life? Sold twice as a mere slave, falsely accused of rape by Potiphar's wife, and now head overseer of the prison's activities! What? How much should one human being have to take in life? The nerve of God to say, "But there in jail GOD was still with Joseph" and "Whatever he did (while in prison) GOD made sure it worked out for the best." *What kind of Kool Aid does the author of Genesis want you and I to drink?* This story is downright depressing. In fact, it almost makes me a little ticked off if you want to know the truth. I can hear you saying that! I feel it as I am writing. It is just not fair for Joseph to be a human pawn in a cosmic chess game called *Life.* Would it make your day to know that "The head jailer gave you free rein, never even checked on you, because GOD was with you?" We don't live in that world, not in America today. Such outlandish hurt, pain, frustration, and betrayal would cause anyone to question the hand of God or even curse God and die as Job's wife suggested for such brutal offenses.

For the next thirteen years, Joseph (he was seventeen when arrested) would find himself in prison for a crime of which he was innocent. Forgotten, displaced, lonely, confused, and hurting, Joseph lived in a red hot, molten season. Gold and silver? Refinery process? Extreme brokenness? *The Fire Factor?* God, really? It just does not add up! Not to me and not to you! Where is God in the midst of Joseph's questions about injustice, extreme suffering, colossal despair, discrete loneliness and unending pain. Joseph had no idea he would ever be released from his prison cell. Day-after-day, month-after-month, year-after-year, the *Fire* raged. I guess that is why this is one of my favorite Bible stories. It makes no sense to every Reader who is thinking in the Natural. The human mind can't connect the dots of God's plan for Joseph's life. I, like you, would have grown weary and despondent. Worse yet, I maybe would have slipped into anger, resentment, bitterness, and hatred of a God who put me in a black-hole kind of life for everyone to gander at, mock at, and ridicule. Come on now, you would say the same thing! Joseph was experiencing some "heavy stuff", as we would see it! Who would want to be in Joseph's shoes? I think we would all pass on that opportunity. Yes, that line to switch places would be a very short line, at least at this point in the story.

Whew! Thank God, the story of Joseph's life does not end this way. Yes, Joseph started in a *pit*, then moved onto a *prison*, but, in the end, Joseph was rubbing shoulders with Pharaoh in the *Palace* in Egypt as the second-in-Command. You heard me right! *Joseph went from the pit, to the prison, to ultimately landing back in the Palace.* What? How can this be? What changed for Joseph? Our boy, Joseph, ends up as the second in power in the nation of Egypt, directly under the Pharaoh. I am *not* making this stuff up. This story is recorded in Genesis 41:38-43, "³⁸ Then Pharaoh said to his officials, "Isn't this the man we need? *Are we going to find anyone else who has God's spirit in him like this?"* ³⁹⁻⁴⁰ So Pharaoh said to Joseph, "You're the man for us. God has given you the inside story—no one is as qualified as you in experience and wisdom. From now on, you're in charge of my affairs; *all my people will report to you.* Only as king will I be over you." ⁴¹⁻⁴³ So Pharaoh commissioned Joseph: *"I'm putting you in charge of the entire country of Egypt."* Then Pharaoh removed his signet ring from his finger and slipped it on Joseph's hand. He outfitted him in robes of the best linen and put a gold chain around his neck. He put the second-in-command chariot at his disposal, and as he rode people shouted "Bravo!" Joseph was in charge of the entire Country of Egypt. (MSG). BRAVO, to GOD!

My Dear Friend, where do you think Joseph learned his insights on how to lead? How could the Pharaoh say, "no one is as qualified as you in experience and wisdom?" Did Joseph stumble upon this understanding, knowledge, and leadership savvy? Absolutely not! As you recall, Joseph started out as a puffed-up, cocky young youngster with a big mouth! He made sure his brothers knew of his status and acclaim. Yet, God had some refining to do in Joseph's life to get him ready for what lay ahead, second-in-Command under Pharaoh. God know where Joseph's life was headed and what was necessary as a foundation to sustain it. Yes, God did use life's hardships, misfortunes, blunders, and challenges to transform Joseph into a humble, servant of the Lord and ultimately the Pharaoh. No longer was Joseph tooting his own horn. He was willing to be used in a manner that God would gain Glory. In the end, God was always in control, while at times, it looked as though He had forgotten about Joseph. Even so, Joseph recognized the hand of God and shared with his brothers some of the most famous lines in all the Bible as declared in Genesis 50:15-20, "[15] When Joseph's brothers saw that their father was dead, they said, "What if Joseph holds a grudge against us and pays us back for all the wrongs we did to him?" [16] So they sent word to Joseph, saying, "Your father left these instructions before he died: [17] 'This is what you are to say to Joseph: *I ask you to forgive your brothers the sins and the wrongs they committed in treating you so badly.*' Now please forgive the sins of the servants of the God of your father." When their message came to him, *Joseph wept.* [18] His brothers then came and threw themselves down before him. "We are your slaves," they said. [19] But Joseph said to them, *"Don't be afraid. Am I in the place of God? [20] You intended to harm me, but God intended it for good to accomplish what is now being done, the saving of many lives. [21]* So then, don't be afraid. I will provide for you and your children." And he reassured them and spoke kindly to them."

Wow! I never get tired of reading that final portion of the book of Genesis. It is so rich with nuggets of gold for real life and relational health. We see such confidence in Joseph that God had a master plan that transcended their evil actions and the God of the Bible turns things around for the good of those who are earnestly seeking Him for direction and support. Joseph had years to think about what God was up to and though he didn't understand all the specifics,

Joseph knew God purposed this for the saving of many lives. That is *amazing* to me! God brought *The Fire Factor* to Joseph's life and, in the end, Joseph is reunited with his brothers, forgives them completely, acknowledges God's sovereign hand on the whole thing, and assures his brothers of a better life, there in Egypt.

That is the making of a great Disney story, "And they lived happily ever after". God brought triumph from tragedy. He brought joy from sorrow. He brought healing from hate. He brought purpose from pain. He brought faith from frustration. He brought conviction from correction. He brought strength from weakness. He brought prominence from obscurity. He brought position from patience. Should I go on? I think you get the message. Through the right lens, we see clearly what God does in one's life and while it looks as though it is flying out of control, God is crafting an "Epic Story" of a life, through time, testing, tragedy, and truth. *Joseph emerged a Hero of the Christian Faith.*

God is still doing such things today in the lives of countless people! He has not given up on this tactic for it works so effectively. *Fire brings heat and heat brings change!* Enough said! It worked in Joseph and it will work in you, too. No matter the situation or proverbial country side of life, God can turn it around for your Good. The Bible paints such a Heavenly backdrop of life through this Word in Romans 8:28, "And we know that in <u>all</u> things God works for the good of those who love Him, who have been called according to His purpose." (NIV)

What are you facing today? Where do you currently reside: the pit, the prison, or the palace? Where has life taken you? Have you been sold to the highest bidder? Have you been falsely accused of a crime you did not commit? Are you living with favor from the head prison guard? Have you been forgotten in the prison as others exit before you, as Joseph did? Do you sense God has abandoned you and left you to figure out this mess called *Life*? Does it look as though all hope is gone and chances of a better life seem *impossible*? Then, I challenge you to go back and reread Genesis, Chapters 37 – 50, for yourself. Please allow Joseph's life to be your poster child for a *Turn It Around* in your life. Nothing is too hard for God, *absolutely nothing!* While it may not happen as fast as we like, God is always working on our behalf to take us from the pit, through the prison, and ultimately to the palace. Are you ready? God's ready? Keep moving. I used to listen to this song while in high school. It would always encourage me to "Keep on Trucking" in life, despite the hurdles. I had no idea of its relevance to every day living and personal growth. The group was named after a fire engine called: Reo Speedwagon and the song was "Keep Pushin", one of my favorites back then. Here is the chorus that we can all relate to:

(Keep pushin', keep pushin', keep pushin')
Keep pushin' on
(Keep pushin', keep pushin', keep pushin')
You know you have got to, got to, be so strong
(Keep pushin', keep pushin', keep pushin')
Well even if you think, your strength is gone
(Keep pushin', keep pushin')
Keep pushin' on

As we move into the next Chapter, God sees your end from the beginning. He has a Master portrait of your life and He will work in you to create such divine beauty. Your part is simple and yet profound, all at the same time. Just, *Keep Pushing on!* If you think things look helpless? *Keep Pushing on.* If you want to give up and quit? *Keep Pushing on.* If you are tired and weary? *Keep Pushing on.* Do you get the picture? *Keep Pushing on.*

It's Your Move!

1. Purity is lost in our modern culture. Why do you think God is so focused on your purity? _____

    _____

    _____.

2. Character, conduct, communication, convictions, and connections. How do you rate yourself in each area? 0 is low and 10 is high. Score each area. How can you improve?

3. Righteousness. God still cares about this. What do you think about this in your life? How are you doing? _____

    _____

    _____.

4. What have you learned from the life of Joseph now?

    a._____

    b._____

    c._____

    d._____.

12

Can I Get a Witness?

Thanks for making it thus far. I know Chapters 9, 10, and 11 were tough chapters to read, ponder, digest, and implement. I assure you that they were equally hard to write because they are pivotal ideas in your life's direction. I equate it to taking the cough medicine that tastes horrible, but know the ultimate end is to make you feel better. Sometimes, the needed and necessary tools and truths are like that *nasty* cough medicine. At the end of the day, they produce the desired effect. Up till now, it is unpleasant to swallow.

Even with God trying to move you in the direction of His best, *Life* seems hard and heartbreaking, at times. However, in retrospect, you will be glad you arrived at your new destination. The Bible calls this "training or discipline" as found in Hebrews 12: 7 – II,

"⁷ Endure hardship as discipline; God is treating you as his children. For what children are not disciplined by their father? ⁸ If you are not disciplined—and everyone undergoes discipline—then you are not legitimate, not true sons and daughters at all. [9] Moreover, we have all had human fathers who disciplined us and we respected them for it. How much more should we submit to the Father of spirits and live! [10] They disciplined us for a little while as they thought best; but God disciplines us for our good, in order that we may share in his holiness. [11] *No discipline seems pleasant at the time, but painful. Later on, however, it produces a harvest of righteousness and peace for those who have been trained by it."* (NIV)

In this chapter, I am going to return to a funny story and illustrate to you how God takes your trials and gives you a *stage* to encourage and comfort others in their daily walk of life. The Bible calls this being a witness. I know you can relate to what the word witness means. We've all watched CSI and Judge Judy on television. Sometimes, people are placed in witness protection programs because their testimony is very impactful and crucial to a case.

Interestingly enough, your testimony is powerful and essential to God and His plan for humanity. He needs you to share with the world around you of His goodness, faithfulness, loving-kindness, mercy and grace. Testimonies transform lives. You have one! Unique to you, but explosive to the masses. God has called you to shine around you and produce heavenly light. As His witness, you matter! Since we can all relate to being a witness on some level, let's kick the tires a bit on what God has in mind as His masterpiece as we drive through *Life*. Are you ready?

Speaking of tires, let me share a story with you involving some tractor tires and a plow. This story speaks to situations where life may find you and your witness becomes the message of the moment. In any and every event, we are a living billboard, being observed by those we influence. I know that might be exciting for you or it might want to make you throw up. Nonetheless, life has a way of throwing a monkey wrench at you in a hurry. Let me share one story that came back to me. *Don't laugh too hard. You might split your pants. It is a true one.*

As mentioned earlier in the book, I was a city boy, through and through. However, my first career season found me in a rural farm community in northeast Georgia in a town called Lavonia. You guess it. It was *"Country"* to the bone. Chicken houses abound, farm land expanses, pick-up truck taxi's and country music anthems. Yes, I felt like a fish out of water and I knew it and it showed! As my first real career offering, I had <u>no</u> intention of staying in this place for very long, I can assure you of that. At least, that is what I told myself to bring a little peace of mind. I got so tired of hearing "You're not from around here, Are Ya?" To which I would ask, "What gave me away. I need to know!" In any event, life marched on and years began to pass by. Through the progression of time (about two years in the making), I ended up marrying one of the local girls. I can testify that I didn't move to this small town with that mindset, but I did tie the knot with the town "princess" with the royal family name. Thankfully, it was not a shotgun wedding, by no means. Nevertheless, I was unprepared for what lay ahead in this *Country Kingdom.*

As is true to God's sense of humor, my new family members were chicken farmers. They had five chicken houses with a total of 80,000 hens. These hens laid eggs twice a day and that made for a lot of eggs moving up the conveyors to the packer. It was quite a set-up. Nearby, there were two large bodies of water which they simply called "the lagoon", pronounced "law-goon" with lots of southern drawl. I think these two sewage holes surfaced as a setting of the loch ness monster in the 1980's. *No, I'm kidding.* At least, that is the rumor I heard while dating. Just a little farm humor for the moment. Ha-Ha.

In any event, the lagoon served to help with chicken manure removal and funky smell reduction. To be honest, I didn't go near the lagoon on a regular basis, but it was near the chicken houses and visible (to the watering eyes). And, exceedingly noticeable to the nose!

In addition, my new family had large amounts of land on which they would plant the annual family garden and harvested their vegetables to can and store for later years. It was just like classic country living, right out of the *Country Music Television* (CMT) vaults. I felt a little weird most of the time in this season of my life, but I found favor in the eyes of the father-in-law. That's kind of like when Joseph found favor in the eyes of the head prison guard. I was certainly open to learning new things about my emerging country world experience. Overalls, cat-head biscuits, 4-wheel drive, farm equipment auctions, shotgun cleaning sessions, deer hunting excursions, fried green tomatoes, and the Country Music Association awards were surrounding my city boy landscape. I was knee deep in and I knew it.

One spring season, my father-in-law found himself in the hospital after yet another heart attack. Unable to tackle the demands of farm life and the colossal farming agenda, I took it upon myself to do a good deed for my father-in-law and the family, as a whole. As was the custom every spring, the yearly garden soil needed to be prepared. Having been on a farm with my grandfather in rural Buffalo (you have to go out a way, I admit that), I was not *totally* amiss of farming things. I've seen a tractor. I've touched tractor attachments. I held a degree in mechanical engineering. Come on! *How hard can this stuff be?* I managed to get the plow hooked up to the tractor after several tries of forward and reverse driving. *I was ready to roll!*

Feeling pretty good about myself, I headed out toward the untapped countryside. Yes, hard ground was about to be flipped over like poetry in motion. I started on the far end of the field and dropped the plow. I soon adjusted my speed and had a good mix of power and performance. Can you believe it? I was plowing. I was on the tractor conquering this country-living dirt! I felt so manly, so proud to be a country boy stand-in. Yee-Haw! John Denver's theme song rang in my head. I plowed most of the day in wide open spaces and simply let the tractor and plow dance continue. No worries, No fuss, No fear, Not a care in the world. Thinking I am making brownie points, I head up toward the chicken house and the surrounding lagoon. My joy-riding tractor moments brought me a sense of country contentment and peaceful memories of my childhood.

All that started to change in an instant. In my lapse of attention while basking in my county victory, I never noticed the lagoon fast approaching. I knew in my mind I would need to turn *well* before the lagoon. *I knew that! I knew that! I knew that!* As I approached the lagoon in bullet-like fashion, I started to turn the front wheels of the tractor, just like you would if you were steering a car. *To my utter amazement, nothing happened.* I kept moving toward the lagoon. I turned the steering wheel even *harder.* At this point, the front tires were beginning to bounce up-and-down on the ground (like a basketball), lifting the front end of the tractor. *I promise you I am not making this up.* I began to panic inside. All I could think about was trying to explain to my father-in-law how his "every option" Ford tractor, ended up in the bottom of his chicken lagoon hole. I had fearful visions of swimming to the side of this bird-feather manure recycling pond.

In that moment, my heart began to pound out of my chest. I was heading straight toward the lagoon and I didn't know how to stop. When I tried to apply the brakes, nothing happened. I didn't have the power to depress the brake to make it stop. I stood up from the seat, applying my full weight upon the brake pedal. Nothing happened, again! Shock came over my body. I honestly didn't know what to do any longer. *I was panic-stricken.* I was moving head-long toward the lagoon and clueless as to how to bring the tractor to a stand still.

In a hail Mary prayer, I asked God to help me. What happened next will be worth the price of this book. *God instantly spoke into my spirit for me to lift up the plow from the dirt.* Quickly, I pulled the lever to lift up the plow. At once, I had the power to press the brake. Straightaway, the front end-stopped bouncing. Suddenly, the brakes were bringing to a stop this massive mechanical monster called a tractor. To my surprise, and utter astonishment, the front tires were at the crest of the incline of the lagoon, ready to make the descent into the *horrid* and *smelly* water. The tractor was saved. I was saved. My marital neck was saved. My reputation was saved. My emotional and mental health was saved. In the blink of an eye, God said to "lift up the plow" from the dirt. It worked. It worked. It worked!

You may be wondering "How does that apply to real life situations and being a witness?" Little did I know that my former father-in-law's land backed up to the home where two of the students we were trying to mentor in our church youth group lived. Both of these young men were in less-than-ideal family dynamics and I had been trying to build a bridge to their lives that was practical, relevant, and timely. The eldest son came running out into the field yelling, "Bud is on the tractor. Bud is on the tractor!" Screaming at the top of his lungs, he was trying to get my attention as all of this *craziness* was unfolding. My high school student friend knew I was in trouble and was running out to help me. How did he know I was heading for calamity that day? That is an easy question. The short answer. *He was watching!* You heard me right. He was watching me plow the field that day.

Why would a seventeen-year-old young man watch me plow the field? On a Saturday with lots of other possibilities and options afforded to him! Where was my student friend? He was watching. Free to get in his car and cruise the local hangouts, watch the latest movies on the cable TV, or play some sports. Yes! But, this day, he was watching. Boredom? Maybe. Reality show called "City Boy Drowns Tractor"? Not Likely. Don't miss this my Dear Friend as it holds in its grip a nugget of gold to consider, "Why was he watching?" Me, of all people? Me?

News flash! They are watching you, too. Everywhere. They are. Every day. On the job. In the traffic. Pumping your gas at the convenience store. Buying diapers at the grocery store. Grilling out at the park. Heading down the road to church. Boating on the lake.

Yup! Your being examined like a hawk. It's who we are. It's what we do. Truthfully, *everyone* is a people watcher, at some point in his, or her, life. We make sport of eyeing people. We do! We really do. We sit on park benches and notice those passing by. We comment. We gesture. We compare. We wonder.

Why? Why? Why? We are curious creatures. We want to know what is the essence of someone's life. What makes him or her unique? What makes someone tick? What makes their lives a witness of a *bigger* story? A Divine story. God's Story?

My student friend wondered too. He was not bashful about it either. He fastened his eyes on me that day and glued his gaze at a would-be city boy fumbling at his attempt to be a farm hand. However, it was *more* than that. My student friend wanted to know are you the *"Real Deal"*. When the dust settles, does your faith work? Can you guide me to a better existence and fuller pathway? You see he, and his younger brother, had to go home to a setting with many challenges. It was bold and it was obvious. My student friend needed *grit* to survive, much less to thrive. Yes, he was watching, alright.

The months that followed that encounter turned brighter for my student buddy. We struck up a friendship deeper than before. At our local youth meetings, I became the brunt of many tractor jokes and southern living jabs. I could take it. It made everyone muse. Among the roar of laughter and heckling, I connected with my student friend, now. He connected with me, too. Why? He was watching that day. My student friend was watching, intently!

Me, a witness? Really? I was no poster child for Christian perfection. Not me. Yet, in my daily pursuit of God and my willingness to grow in my authentic faith, *my Student buddy saw Jesus.* He encountered random glimpses of my Savior. I was no saint by any means. Nevertheless, my friend briefly touched the Divine and it moved him. That was God's goal. A tangible witness for Jesus Christ.

As we move on to Chapter 13, we'll dig deep into a story that will be used as the backdrop for the remainder of this book. Rach, Shach, and Benny are center stage in their life's biggest drama and they are given a chance to be a witness for God. Let's get into their story as we dive into Chapter 13.

"In the same way, let your light shine before others, that they may see your good deeds and glorify your Father in heaven." Matthew 5:16 (NIV)

It's Your Move!

I. Being a Witness. Do you agree that people are watching your life? _____. What would others say about your life? _____.

2. My student friend was watching me. Why do you think he was so intent on viewing my life?

    _____

    _____.

3. My tractor story was funny. Can you relate to doing something that turns out bad? _____

    _____.

4. Does your life inspire others? _____.
    Why or why not? _____.

5. "Let your light so shine before men, that they may see your good works, and glorify your Father which is in heaven." Matthew 5:16 (KJV). Are you shining? _____

    How? _____.

13

Rach, Shach, and Benny

I just love to say the title of this chapter. Rach, Shach, and Benny. Three cool dudes from a distant land. Three courageous partners willing to stand up for God. Three Rockstars of the Christian faith who looked death in the eye and came forth as Heavenly spokesmen. Rach, Shach, and Benny were the character's names I learned about when my young children got hooked on Veggie Tales in the early 2000's. You heard me right, Veggie Tales! We all related to these guys. They were God-fearing vegetables from a by-gone era showcasing the potent truths of Scripture. RSB, the *Hebrew Boy Band* of the Daniel days, were front and center with real life on their heels.

Scared? Yes! Confused? Maybe! Passive? Never! Willing to die? Absolutely!

As with any program of a child's liking, we watched this 30-minute gala of truth over and over again. *Larry the Cucumber* and *Bob the Tomato* were hosts to Rach, Shach, and Benny marathons in our home. Why? We all enjoy stories with abundant promise. We love the death-defying heroics of these Hebrew dynamos. Small in stature, but valiant beyond their years, our daring buddies spoke up for God in a *big* way as found in Daniel 3:1-30 (NLT),

"**3** King Nebuchadnezzar made a gold statue ninety-feet tall and nine-feet wide and set it up on the plain of Dura in the province of Babylon.[2] Then he sent messages to the high officers, officials, governors, advisers, treasurers, judges, magistrates, and all the provincial officials to come to the dedication of the statue he had set up. [3] So all these officials came and stood before the statue King Nebuchadnezzar had set up.

[4] Then a herald shouted out, "People of all races and nations and languages, listen to the king's command! [5] When you hear the sound of the horn, flute, zither, lyre, harp, pipes, and other musical instruments, bow to the ground to worship King Nebuchadnezzar's gold statue.[6] *Anyone who refuses to obey will immediately be thrown into a blazing (fiery) furnace.*"

[7] So at the sound of the musical instruments, all the people, whatever their race or nation or language, bowed to the ground and worshiped the gold statue that King Nebuchadnezzar had set up.

[8] But some of the astrologers went to the king and informed on the Jews. [9] They said to King Nebuchadnezzar, "Long live the king! [10] You issued a decree requiring all the people to bow down and worship the gold statue when they hear the sound of the horn, flute, zither, lyre, harp, pipes, and other musical instruments. [11] That decree also states that those who refuse to obey must be thrown into a blazing furnace.[12] But there are some Jews—*Shadrach, Meshach, and Abednego*— whom *you* have put in charge of the province of Babylon. *They pay no attention to you, Your Majesty. They refuse to serve your gods and do not worship the gold statue you have set up.*"

[13] Then Nebuchadnezzar flew into a rage and ordered that Shadrach, Meshach, and Abednego be brought before him. When they were brought in, [14] Nebuchadnezzar said to them, "Is it true,

Shadrach, Meshach, and Abednego, that you refuse to serve my gods or to worship the gold statue I have set up? *15 I will give you one more chance to bow down and worship the statue I have made when you hear the sound of the musical instruments. But if you refuse, you will be thrown immediately into the blazing furnace.* <u>And then what god will be able to rescue you from my power?"</u>

16 Shadrach, Meshach, and Abednego replied, "O Nebuchadnezzar, *we do not need to defend ourselves before you. 17 If we are thrown into the blazing (fiery) furnace, the God whom we serve is able to save us. He will rescue us from your power, Your Majesty. 18 <u>But</u> even if he doesn't, we want to make it clear to you, Your Majesty, that we will <u>never</u> serve your gods or worship the gold statue you have set up."*

19 Nebuchadnezzar was so furious with Shadrach, Meshach, and Abednego *that his face became distorted with rage.* He commanded that the furnace be heated *seven* times hotter than usual. 20 Then he ordered some of the strongest men of his army to *bind* Shadrach, Meshach, and Abednego and throw them into the blazing furnace. *21 So they tied them up and threw them into the furnace, fully dressed in their pants, turbans, robes, and other garments.* 22 And because the king, in his anger, had demanded such a hot fire in the furnace, the flames killed the soldiers as they threw the three men in. *23 So Shadrach, Meshach, and Abednego, securely tied, fell into the roaring flames.*

24 But suddenly, Nebuchadnezzar jumped up in amazement and exclaimed to his advisers, "Didn't we tie up three men and throw them into the furnace?"

"Yes, Your Majesty, we certainly did," they replied.

25 *"Look!" Nebuchadnezzar <u>shouted</u>. "I see four men, unbound, walking around in the fire unharmed! And the fourth looks like a god!" (some translations say "the Son of God)*

26 Then Nebuchadnezzar came as close as he could to the door of the flaming furnace and shouted: "Shadrach, Meshach, and Abednego, servants of *the Most High God*, come out! Come here!"

So, Shadrach, Meshach, and Abednego stepped out of the fire. [27] Then the high officers, officials, governors, and advisers crowded around them and saw that the fire had not touched them. *Not a hair on their heads was singed, and their clothing was not scorched. They didn't even smell of smoke!*

[28] Then Nebuchadnezzar said, "Praise to the God of Shadrach, Meshach, and Abednego! He sent his angel to rescue his servants who trusted in him. *They defied the king's command and were willing to die rather than serve or worship any god except their own God.* [29] Therefore, I make this decree: If any people, whatever their race or nation or language, speak a word against the God of Shadrach, Meshach, and Abednego, they will be torn limb from limb, and their houses will be turned into heaps of rubble. *There is no other god who can rescue like this!"*

[30] Then the king <u>promoted</u> Shadrach, Meshach, and Abednego to even higher positions in the province of Babylon."

Wow! *Real Life* stories don't get any weightier than that. I added a few bold highlights, underlines, along with some italics of my own to point out a few of the best parts of this heavenly drama. If you have never read this or have not read it in a while, you can't help but wonder of the heroics of such committed men. A fiery furnace would make us all evaluate our faith and our devotion to it. Yet, in the face of death, the King gave them no wiggle room or compromise. Worship the statue or die! How is that for a Plan A or Plan B edict. Plan A gives them a life saving option. How easy it would have been to say "yes" to the King and bow a knee in reverence and homage. To surrender to this earthly King would have been a blemish of loyalty to their dedication to the King of Kings, Jesus Christ. Shadrach, Meshach, and Abednego, as they are officially called, were not willing to dishonor or disown their commitment with the God of their ancestors Abraham, Isaac, and Jacob. Bravery on steroids or foolishness as it were, they were triumphantly given to Plan B, "Die for their faith in God".

Marvin Robert Wohlhueter, Th.D.

This story can't help but cause us to evaluate our own convictions about faith and practice. Sunday morning service...I'm in. Read my Bible regularly, Sure thing! Give to the poor at Thanksgiving or serve the homeless at a nearby soup kitchen. With joy. Visit the elderly. Often. A fiery furnace? A Human bar-b-que? A torched tostado? You get the picture. Rach, Shach, and Benny didn't ask the King for a few minutes to pray about the situation. They didn't ask for a life-line to a family member for some quick advice. These Hebrew blokes, without a second of hesitation, sealed their fate with a fiery furnace decree, "We will not bow to your statue!"

Put yourself in their shoes! What would you have done? Relive their story with *you* as the main character. If your life was on the line, would you give in to the pressure to bow to the King? Would you bow publicly and then later ask God for forgiveness privately? *While death is scary, denial is permanent.* Jesus said it this way in Matthew 10:33 (NLT), "³³ But all who stand before others and say they do not believe in me, I will say before my Father in heaven that they do not belong to me." Jesus gives no wiggle room just like the King did for Rach, Shach, and Benny as he gave no wiggle room. They were at a crossroad of faith. Two roads? Yes! But, only one Master wins.

It grips the human heart in a very *real* way. A yes to one is a no to the other. That is the way it has always been, even in ancient Bible days. Nevertheless, for the captive youths, death was a welcomed friend if their God was to be glorified by this act of surrender. Would you have done the same?

Real Life creates similar crossroads. A *Yes* to one decision is a no to another. A *Yes* to honor God is a no to feed the body with its carnal desires. A *Yes* to live for righteousness is a no to live for political correctness. A *Yes* to stand for truth is a no to agree with society's reasoning. Like Rach, Shach, and Benny, you can't straddle the fence or even stand on the fence, for that matter. We live in precarious times and God is waiting for you to engage the culture with Divine authority and a humble spirit. The Word of God gives us a unique pictorial contrast, but it makes perfect descriptive sense as found in Matthew 10:16, "¹⁶ "Listen, I am sending you out like sheep among wolves. *So be as clever as snakes and as innocent as doves."*

Could it be that Rach, Shach, and Benny were living out this snake and dove's storyline? I think they were and we get the pleasure of their life-changing tale. Let's unpack their story in microscopic detail in the chapters that follow. Together, we can glean specific nuggets of truth to apply to our lives. God has a grand future for you and the Brother's RSB can surely testify that in <u>all</u> things God's got your back...Even in a fiery furnace. Chapter 14, here we come.

It's Your Move!

1. Rach, Shack, and Benny. Have you ever heard of the story? Having now read it, how does it impact you? _____

    _____

    _____.

2. Live or die? How would you have responded? _____

    _____

    _____.

3. Political Correctness? Yes or no? Do you operate with God's truth? _____

    _____.

4. "16 "Listen, I am sending you out like sheep among wolves. So be as clever as snakes and as innocent as doves." List three steps to take in light of this story! a. _____

    _____ b. _____

    _____ c. _____

    _____.

14

Through the Looking Glass

I loved Christmas time as a child. I guess most children do. I lived in Buffalo, New York as a youngster where "Dreaming of a White Christmas" was not necessary. Buffalo measured snow in feet, not inches as they do in Atlanta, Georgia which I now call home. As a kid, my parents played a fun game at Christmas time. They used to call it "Seek-a-Peek". We would always have one present that my mom and dad would pick out for each of the four children. Then, they would allow us to look through a small hole, up close, just to get a glimpse of the beloved gift awaiting its Christmas arrival. You could imagine it only heightened the sense of excitement and anticipation of Christmas. Most times, we would never guess the gift because the peep hole was so small we could not make out the details. Nonetheless, the game made the season electric and whimsical. Close your eyes. Can you see the candy canes and the tinsel on the tree? Do you smell the aroma of fresh Christmas pine trees? Do you see the lights ushering in the season? As I write this chapter, we are just weeks away from the Christmas celebration once again. I love this time of year.

My seek-a-peek game from yester year can lend itself well into the story of Rach, Shach, and Benny. The title of this chapter gives you a word picture to ponder: *Looking Glass*. Have you ever heard the term before? Have you ever seen one? From the dictionary, the following definitions are found: 1. (n) a glass used as a mirror. 2. (adj) with normal or familiar circumstances reversed; topsy-turvy. Both ingredients of the definition will help us to examine the backstory of Shadrach, Meshach, and Abednego. These ingredients will also give you tools to examine your own backstory.

The noun of the Looking Glass introduces a dual application for such a device. Picture if you will a clear glass. If you are up close, the glass permits one to look through and see in limited fashion the object under consideration. In conjunction to that, if you pull back far enough, the Looking Glass now becomes a mirror-like tool which gives you a glimpse of self. To recap, up close, you see through the glass at the object with diminished viewing, but enough to seek-a-peek. When you step back a few feet, you see your own reflection. Singular in construction. Dual in purpose. Divinely helpful!

The Looking Glass effect is influential because that is much how life works. We look through the glass with limited understanding and insight. We get seek-a-peek moments every day. Nevertheless, we then have to take a few steps back to get a reflection view of ourselves and ponder what we see. Now, I am not talking about hair and make-up, clean teeth, or a dashing outfit. Look deeper into the Looking Glass. What you see, with spiritual eyes, is more important than what you see with natural eyes. The Apostle Paul said words closely paralleling this as declared in I Corinthians 13:12 (NIV), "12 For now we see only a reflection as in a mirror; then we shall see face to face. Now I know in part; then I shall know fully, even as I am fully known."

The Looking Glass had a descriptive flare to it as well. An adjective is a clarifying word as you remember from English class. For example, the red ball bounced down the driveway. In this instance, red helps us envision the ball with more precision. Shadrach, Meshach, and Abednego were living a Looking Glass life. Topsy-turvy? Yes. Normal or familiar circumstances reversed. A hearty amen to that! No one signs up for a Looking Glass kind of life. You would not. Neither would I. However, like the RSB Brothers learned, *Life* has a way of crafting those types of outcomes. Helpful? Impactful? Necessary? Why?

Every day of your life, you are looking into a seek-a-peek dynamic. You have limited insight and understanding about an event, action, or behavior. You get up as close as the Looking Glass permits. With squinted eyes, you peer into the dilemma with a heart to learn, grow, and benefit. Yes, with every ounce of your being, you try to be strong, brave, and hopeful. Shaking your head, you take a few steps back. Now, the Looking Glass touts your reflection. You see with natural eyes, at first. Fuzzy, unfocused, and questionable, you try to make sense of it all. What could this mean? What should I do now? Can I make it through? Why would my life be heading in this direction? All fair questions to consider. All quite troubling.

Looking Glasses don't always write the scripts to our liking. Take the fiery furnace colleagues. One morning, they wake up with a flurry of promise. Hit the ground running with daily demands. In a matter of hours, the Looking Glass effect changed everything. Rach, Shach, and Benny were summoned to the King's court. Oblivious to the threat at-hand, the King wants to know why they have chosen to ignore his pronouncement to worship the golden statue. Everyone else has. Why should you be any different? With the kindness of his kingly heart, he gives them another chance to fall in line. Seems reasonable. Bow and live. Go with the crowd and save your lives. With people watching, the temperature in the room heats up, no pun intended. The King is used to getting his way. He always has. King Nebby does not have to play by the rules. In fact, he makes the rules. Rach, Shach, and Benny were testing his patience. Who says the Bible is not comical, at times, as found in Daniel 3:19 (NLT)," [19] Nebuchadnezzar was so furious with Shadrach, Meshach, and Abednego that his face became distorted with rage."

Can you visualize the face of the King? Can you ponder the boldness of these God-fearing brothers? *One face riddled with anger. Three faces softened with peace. One face heavy with mischief. Three faces resolute with conviction. One face determined to win. Three faces content to die.* Looking Glass moments can bring out the best and the worst in all of us. Distorted or purposeful? *You get to choose your face today!* That is why the Looking Glass requires you to take a few steps back and see your reflection. Life can hit you hard, but it does not have to <u>distort</u> you. Life can slow you down, but it does not have to knock you out. Life can cause you to wonder, but it does not have to make you give up. I think a key scripture that speaks to this point is found in Proverbs 24:16 (NIV), "[16] for though the righteous fall seven times, *they rise again*, but the wicked stumble when calamity strikes."

Everyone falls. Sometimes often. But, the righteous rise again. Did you catch that? Falling is not a fatality. Staying down is optional. God summons you to *Get Up!* Dust yourself off. And, get back in the game. Could it be that our Looking Glass flashes are designed to see what we are really made of? Might they help us to define the truly important things in life? Would it not be wonderful for Looking Glass moments to remove the superficial <u>fluff</u> of life and guide us to a healthier view of living?

For Shadrach, Meshach, and Abednego, they were knocking on death's door, literally. Talk about a topsy-turvy morning for the Hebrew brothers. They must have had a double shot of java jolt that morning to utter such convicting words to the King as found in Daniel 3:16-18 (NIV), "[16] Shadrach, Meshach and Abednego replied to him, "King Nebuchadnezzar, we do not need to defend ourselves before you in this matter. [17] If we are thrown into the blazing furnace, the God we serve is able to deliver us from it, and he will deliver us from Your Majesty's hand. *[18] But even if he does not, we want you to know, Your Majesty, that we will not serve your gods or worship the image of gold you have set up.*"

In this audacious moment, good and evil squared off for a heavenly knock-down battle. Gripping as it were, we know the outcome quickly as we read the Bible. Rach, Shach, and Benny didn't know what hung in the balance. Take a few minutes and consider this battle. *Will vs. Wit? Muscle vs. Mind? Heaven vs. Hell?* What would you do in their shoes? *Really?* Dive into the story! You face consequences of momentous proportions, too. It may not cost you your life, but there is a cost, nonetheless. God is growing your level of boldness as you aspire to be more like Him. Consider the words of Jesus as found in the Gospel of Matthew 10:39 (NIV), "[39] Whoever finds their life will lose it, and whoever loses their life for my sake will find it." *Could it be that living only really finds it meaning in God and without God, what do you have to live for? Shadrach, Meshach, and Abednego must have thought the same way. Do You?* Let's move onto Chapter 15 to dig deeper.

It's Your Move!

1. Looking Glass Moments! Describe one that has occurred lately. _____
   _____.

2. How could these Brothers be so calm? _____
   _____
   _____.

3. When you fall, what do you do? _____.
   Do you rise quickly? _____.
   Why or why not? _____.

4. Will vs. Wit, Muscle vs. Mind, Heaven vs. Hell. What would you do if you were in their shoes? List four things
   a. _____.
   b. _____.
   c. _____.
   d. _____.

15

Does This Happen to Everyone?

Candid Camera. Have you heard of it? Have you seen it? I dare you to go to You Tube and search the title. See what you find. You will not stop laughing. That I promise you. I may be dating myself, but I want to share how Candid Camera worked. It will illustrate for you a boundless truth. *Life Happens!*

Candid Camera aired from 1960 to 1976. Its storyline was to construct a scene where unsuspecting people would be thrust into a hilarious dilemma. Little did they know the whole event was being recorded for the viewing audience to watch. The antics of the show provided for some classic entertainment as people waded through the oddity. For example, let's say a person was getting a bottle of apple juice at a local grocery story. The person would pick up one bottle to place into his or her cart and the whole endcap of juice bottles would be triggered to fall. The colossal mess would capture the person's reactions, behavior, and yes, sometimes, language bombs. The person would not be aware that the entire footage was being viewed and recorded. The overwhelming thought of the person is "this can't be real. I don't believe what is happening here". As the audience gets a good laugh, the not-so-lucky participant wonders about the unfolding quandary. At that moment, deep into the humor, the creator and TV host, Allen Funt, would come out to greet the guest, point to where the camera was hidden and say "Smile, You're on Candid Camera". Often, the person would slump down to the ground in relief as if to say, "I'm so glad this is only a put-on". At which point, the contestant might, then, show some humor of his or her own at the "Gotcha" story.

Ironically, during that era, it was not uncommon when something happened so bizarre that one would yell "Smile, you're on Candid Camera". Then, he or she would look around as if to find a camera recording the whole experience. If you are like most, you may think your life is one big Candid Camera show. You scratch your head in disbelief as the daily events unfold. Dishwasher leaks water all over your hardwood floors causing them to buckle. *Big financial LO$$.* You get a letter from the school principal for a parent-teacher meeting because your little Johnny can't stop biting his classmates. *Big embarrassment.* Your sibling seems to have hung the moon relationally and you wonder why your marriage provides less than a stellar outcome. *Big resentment.* You have a teenager on drugs and aging parents in Depends. *Big stress. Big, Big, Big!*

These *Big Life* grenades happen to everyone, believe it or not. You are NOT alone in the blow-out department. This leads us to the Ist Truth of our *Fiery Furnace* story:

1. *Fiery trials are __PART__ of everyday __LIFE__.*

Call it what you want, but real life produces real stuff. You are not odd because your son bites. All young children bite, at times. Dishwashers do break down and cause damage. That's why you have homeowner's insurance. Every marriage has feelings of restlessness and boredom. You are normal here. In today's world, drugs and Depends can ring true for you and many others like you. *So, relax!* God's got your back. What if we took a group of ten people and put them in a room together. Next, we asked them to list their ten top *Life* stressors at the present moment. After this, we gave you the chance to go around the room and read each person's list. Imagine that you could then trade problems with anyone in the room. Would you? Don't dance by this question. What would you learn from such an exercise. *Answer: Everyone has trials, fiery trials.* I suppose you would walk back to the list of your ten stressors, pick them back up and go home, relieved. Why? Because, you can manage your *funk*, but not some of the other's lists.

The Bible speaks to such a situation as found in 2 Corinthians 4:17 (NIV), "17 For our light and momentary troubles are achieving for us an eternal glory that far outweighs them all." Light? I doubt it. Momentary? Hardly. But, the outcome is glorious. The verb here is *achieving* from which we get the word *"achievement"*. Your troubles have an achievement assigned to them. What is that achievement: *Eternal Glory!* Take a deep breath and soak that in. I suspect that maybe for the first time you have now linked your troubles with glory, Eternal Glory. Could it be that God uses fiery trials to generate glorious aftermaths?

Also, noted in the above verse is a measure of comparison. The text says, "far outweighs them all". What? Double for my trouble, maybe. *It might be a 10 to 1 or a 100 to 1 increase.* Who knows the exact number, but nonetheless, the win you get is Heavenly in nature. Press on, My Friend. Know that God's got your back.

If Shadrach, Meshach, and Abednego were honest with us, they might be looking around for cameras and crews in their storyline as well. They were not looking to die that day, but they were sure willing to do so if that's what it took. Would they exclaim that an eternal glory was awaiting them? I think so! Death humbles a person.

However, for the Christian, death in this life is merely a passage way to our glory, Eternal Glory.

Take a few minutes and ask yourself, "Do I recognize that fiery trials are part of my everyday experience?" A key take-away from Rach, Shach, and Benny is that not every fiery trial moment is a result of wrongful doing. These are the ones that are hardest to navigate and understand. Why? *While doing the right thing, you don't expect to encounter trials.* Real life does happen, though. The Hebrew brothers found this out first hand as explained in Daniel 3:12 (NIV), "¹² But there are some Jews whom you have set over the affairs of the province of Babylon—Shadrach, Meshach and Abednego—who pay no attention to you, Your Majesty. They neither serve your gods nor worship the image of gold you have set up."

Honoring God was of first importance to Shadrach, Meshach, and Abednego. Your loyalty to God does not excite every on-looker. The King wanted surrender, but so did God. Consequently, Rach, Shach, and Benny chose to yield to the God of *ALL* Glory. Doing the right thing is always the right answer. Doing the right thing does not always get the *praised* outcome from men. *Yet, God sees!*

Let's make this chapter's ending personal and practical. What are you going through that you feel all alone in? How have you responded? Do you think God is picking on you because your life is so tough to navigate? What Candid Camera scripts do you think you are starring in, lately? If you could trade troubles with another person, would you? Have you ever considered the exchange of Troubles = Eternal Glory?

Before you close your eyes tonight, lay your head on your pillow and say your nightly prayer, pause to thank God for the ways He has been with you during your fiery trial expeditions. Achieving an eternal weight of glory takes time. Ask God to give you the patience to grow during these fiery tests. You are doing way better than you might give yourself credit for. I assure you of that. I would challenge you to pick your top three stressors in the past six months. What has God shown you about yourself in the midst of these irritating times? Now, let's move on to Truth # 2 in the upcoming chapter.

It's Your Move!

1. Candid Camera. You ever heard of it? _____.
   What about this show would be funny? _____
   _____.

2. Do you ever feel like your life is on the show? _____
   Why or why not? _____.
   How has it impacted you? _____.
   _____.

3. Rach, Shack, and Benny were forced to decide. How would you
   respond? _____.
   Do you think God sees the details of your life? _____.
   How do you know? _____.

4. Troubles = Eternal Glory! What troubles are you facing today?
   a. _____ b. _____
   c. _____. How would God want you to
   respond? _____
   _____.

16

Living in a Fish Bowl

A Pastor's Life and Fish Bowl living are synonyms for each other? Yes, that is true. In my early days, when I was called to a small church in Greensboro, NC, my wife (then) was concerned about measuring up to everyone's expectations. No doubt, you place on yourself an invisible burden that wears you down. With each passing day, this cargo becomes heavier as people raise the bar on your life. The Fish Bowl life has its downfall: *Burnout.* Trying to meet everyone's wishes can be exhausting. We both felt the weightiness of on-looking eyes as we tried to execute building a thriving church. Day-by-day, my wife slowly began to check-out emotionally. This leaking of soul and purpose eventually caused us to wonder if we were content doing ministry as a young family. It was tiresome! (Raleigh was just born.)

After six months of developing ministry systems and plans for growth, *I was asked to step down as their Pastor.* The reason was a conflict of interest in where I was taking the vision of the church. I was dismissed one summer evening in late August, 1996. At the time, I didn't know if it was a welcomed relief or a blow to my heart. My wife was glad to stop living in a Fish Bowl lifestyle. As for myself, I was more heart-broken to say the least. Yet, I understood my wife's position. Living the Fish Bowl life can be draining, grueling, and problematic. Why? Everyone is looking at you. And, often! They want to know how you are going to respond to Life's stressors.

Does this sound familiar? Shadrach, Meshach, and Abednego had similar concerns. When the wheels fall off the buggy rolling down a hill at high rates of travel, people tend to stop and watch. When your life hits some tight places, others will stop to watch, too. Such was the case for our Hebrew friends as noted in Daniel 3:13b – 15, "So these men were brought before the king, [14] and Nebuchadnezzar said to them, "Is it true, Shadrach, Meshach and Abednego, that you do not serve my gods or worship the image of gold I have set up? [15] Now when you hear the sound of the horn, flute, zither, lyre, harp, pipe and all kinds of music, if you are ready to fall down and worship the image I made, very good. But if you do not worship it, you will be thrown immediately into a blazing furnace. Then what god will be able to rescue you from my hand?"

This popcorn moment had many spectators, people watchers looking for drama. The tension was thick and the reality of this minute even thicker. This brings us to Truth # 2:

2. *Fiery trials get the whole world <u>LOOKING</u> at you.*

People stare. People wonder. People invade your space. People are naturally curious at someone else's predicament. Sad, but true. When an accident occurs on a local highway, people park their cars and watch the unfolding tragedy. When a home is on fire, people pause to watch the firemen put it out. When a dilemma occurs, people will spend <u>their</u> precious time glancing over the carnage of another's misfortune. Call it what you want, but people like a thrilling storyline. I guess that is why in the last 10 to 15 years, Reality TV has become the big viewing variety of choice. We watch others in tough spots. We watch others in bad situations. We evaluate <u>our</u> lives based on their dysfunction and we feel good about ourselves. Strange!

I recently saw an advertisement for a Reality TV show called *Expecting* (I think that is right?). The story motif is documenting *young* girls that are pregnant planning to give birth. These girls are teenagers, unmarried, unprepared, and unsure about life and it ensuing outcomes. I had to do a double-take as I watched this marketing ploy. Can we be so shallow that we enjoy watching a show where clearly this misfortune is <u>not</u> worthy to be flaunted? You must decide for yourself.

What about a human bar-b-que? People were lined up to watch Rach, Shach, and Benny get cooked by the fiery furnace. All the others bowed their knee. They were now safe. All the others praised the golden statue, readily. Fearing for their life? Probably! Willing to stand out? Not likely. Given to conformity? Without question. Gutsy? Never. People watchers? Every time! *They wished they could have been as bold as Rach, Shach, and Benny, but it's too costly. Death? Just can't do it!*

However, Shadrach, Meshach, and Abednego welcomed death if that's what it meant to be loyal to their God. All eyes were on them. *Talk about Living in a Fish Bowl.* Deep down, the people wanted to believe in these three unsung heroes for their faith. Deep down, they wanted them to rise above this battle of wills. Deep down, the spectators were hoping to witness a Divine miracle. *Guess what? They did!*

God states that Fish Bowl living is OK. It is penned quite boldly in Matthew 5:14-16 (NIV), "¹⁴ "You are the light of the world. A town built on a hill cannot be hidden.¹⁵ Neither do people light a lamp and put it under a bowl. Instead they put it on its stand, and it gives light to everyone in the house. *¹⁶ In the same way, let your light shine before others, that they may see your good deeds and glorify your Father in heaven.*"

Shining lights get noticed. God wants it to be so. When the world presses in, our deeds get put on display. Don't take this time lightly. In this twinkling, God can get glory. Glorifying their Father in heaven was at the top of Shadrach, Meshach, and Abednego's list. *What about your list?*

Living in a Fish Bowl, while not easy, can cause the most personal growth for your life. And, growth is needed! You need it. I need it. We all need it. Check out what is found in 2 Peter 1:5-8 (NIV), "⁵ For this very reason, make every effort to <u>add</u> to your faith *goodness*; and to goodness, *knowledge*; ⁶ and to knowledge, *self-control*; and to self-control, *perseverance*; and to perseverance, *godliness*; ⁷ and to godliness, *mutual affection*; and to mutual affection, *love*. ⁸ *For if you possess these qualities <u>in increasing measure</u>, they will keep you from being <u>ineffective</u> and <u>unproductive</u> in your knowledge of our Lord Jesus Christ."*

Every Fish Bowl experience has at its core the ability to produce the above ingredients. Also, note that the text states to <u>add</u> these "in increasing measure" in the following order:

1. Goodness
2. Knowledge
3. Self-Control
4. Perseverance
5. Godliness
6. Mutual Affection
7. Love

The end game is spelled out undoubtedly, here, "They will keep you from being <u>ineffective</u> and <u>unproductive</u> in your knowledge of our Lord Jesus Christ." Wow! That's it. *Effective and productive lives are at the center of God's heart as it pertains to His Son, Jesus Christ.* Could it be that what was driving Rach, Shach, and Benny was a bedrock fervor to be effective and productive witnesses for God before a foolhardy audience, even in the face of death?

As we move toward the end of this book, the self-reflection times might get a little potent. *Don't take this as meddling or being pushy.*

Now that we have been on this voyage together for a while, it's time to make changes *that heal your past, help in your present, and bring hope to your future.* If you are a follower of Jesus Christ (if not, stop now and consider reading the invitation at the end of this book to know Christ, personally), then, God is trying to <u>add</u> to your faith experience, through fiery troubles, the seven components that make your faith vibrant, alive, and glorious. Don't fight it. Embrace it. And, lean into it! As you enjoy the increasing measure of the seven elements, the spill-over will touch the lives around you. Who could benefit from such a make-over? Yourself? Your spouse? Your children? Your parents? Your employer? Your friends? This list is endless. So is God! And, so is His ability to add the "<u>more</u>" you have been praying for. It is found inside Fish Bowl Living. Just Keep Swimming!

It's Your Move!

1. Living in a Fish Bowl? Have you felt like this? _____.
   What about it makes it so hard? _____
   _____.

2. People Watching! What causes us to stop and watch?
   _____. Do we like
   others to blow it? Be Honest! _____.
   Why? _____.

3. How did our Hebrew Boys respond? _____.
   What can we learn from their actions? _____.
   _____.

4. Reread the seven ingredients God is trying to add to
   your faith. Which three do you need the most right now?
   _____ Why? _____.
   _____.
   Who could benefit from your life changing? _____
   _____.

17

Decisions, Decisions, Decisions

Decisions. Like it or not, your full life is full of them. Big ones. Small ones. Important ones. Silly ones. Life changing ones. Everyday ones. Good ones. Bad ones. Helpful ones. Hurtful ones. You can't escape decisions. *You make them. They make you.* Read these last two sentences again. Do it a third time. Another. One last time. Let's put it below for emphasis:

You Make Them...They Make You!

The decision to drink because of peer pressure: alcoholism. The decision to have premarital sex: pregnancy. The decision to steal: incarceration. The decision to do drugs: addiction. The decision to cheat on a test: expulsion. The decision to have an affair: divorce. The decision to drive while intoxicated: DUI. The decision to avoid a family member: isolation. The decision to hold a grudge:

unforgiveness. The decision to ignore God: lack of purpose. The decision to live without limits: ruin.

You Make Them. . .They Make You! OR, Break you!

We all like to think we are the masters of our own destiny. That simply is not true. God's Word screams otherwise. I can't think of a more appropriate series of Scriptures than Matthew 7: 24-27 (NIV), [24] "Therefore everyone who hears these words of mine and puts them into practice is like a wise man who built his house on the rock. [25] The rain came down, the streams rose, and the winds blew and beat against that house; *yet it did not fall, because it had its foundation on the rock.*[26] But everyone who hears these words of mine and does not put them into practice is like a foolish man who built his house on sand. [27] The rain came down, the streams rose, and the winds blew and beat against that house, *and it fell with a great crash."*

Today, you have a choice. A decision, if you will. Your life can be reduced down to *one* colossal decision. And, you must choose. No one is forcing you to make it. But, *your* world is awaiting <u>the</u> outcome. "Everyone who hears these words of mine and puts them into practice". Jesus cuts to the chase: *Your Foundation will be solid.* Conversely, "Everyone who hears these words of mine and does not put them into practice." Jesus, a second time: *Your Foundation will be shaky.* Here is a definition for shaky:

liable to break down or give way; insecure;
not to be depended upon

Call me crazy, but I can't imagine anyone wanting a shaky foundation in life. However, the evidence is overwhelming that many live with a shaky foundation as they ignore God's directions for their lives. It happens everyday to their destruction. The verse in Joel 3:14 (NIV) paints a vivid picture of the world we live in today,

"Multitudes, multitudes in the valley of decision! For the day of the LORD is near in the valley of decision." This leads us to Truth # 3:

3. *Fiery trials __FORCE__ you to choose sides. Do you believe in God or will you yield to the idols of the world?*

The word picture here grabs me intensely. A valley of decision! We live there, too. Day-in and Day-out. We <u>all</u> live in a Valley of Choices. You are not alone. Multitudes live there, too. Can you visualize a crowded room, shoulder-to-shoulder, front-to-back, bumping into each other? I can! This mammoth audience is carving out a lifestyle. Based on decisions alone, their emerging lives take shape. It's not rocket science, but it is a fact. As we noted earlier, *"You make decisions. . .They make you."*

The Bible is full of people who were at *Life's* crossroads, a fork in the road. An epic example is found in Joshua 24:14 – 18 (NIV), [14] "So fear the LORD and serve him wholeheartedly. Put away forever the idols your ancestors worshiped when they lived beyond the Euphrates River and in Egypt. Serve the LORD alone. [15] But if you refuse to serve the LORD, then choose today whom you will serve. Would you prefer the gods your ancestors served beyond the Euphrates? Or will it be the gods of the Amorites in whose land you now live? *But as for me and my family, we will serve the LORD."*

[16] The people replied, "We would never abandon the LORD and serve other gods. [17] For the LORD our God is the one who rescued us and our ancestors from slavery in the land of Egypt. He performed mighty miracles before our very eyes. As we traveled through the wilderness among our enemies, *he preserved us.* [18] It was the LORD who drove out the Amorites and the other nations living here in the land. *So, we, too, will serve the LORD, for he alone is our God."*

In this classic photograph, the valley of decision was full. The people everywhere were in the crisis: Who will they serve? This <u>one</u> decision impacted *all* other decisions in their lives. Your life is no different, today. Like this patriarch of old shouted, "As for me and my house, we will serve the Lord.", you must arrive at your <u>own</u> outcome, too. Could it be that everything in your life hangs on this one decision? I know what your thinking, "That seems a bit old-fashioned, don't you think?" Not really! Your heart is connected to something, at present. It drives every decision you make. It becomes the backdrop for your life's story. With our mental picture in mind, we forge a life in the present that crafts our future. You must agree that you are now where the series of choices have brought you. You must also agree that if you don't like where you are now, *it will be your choices that will take you out!* That is Good News. *You can "decide" yourself into a better life.*

Think about a life or death decision. Do you have any? Put yourself in Shadrach, Meshach, and Abednego's shoes as the declaration came down as recorded in Daniel 3:4-6 (NIV), "⁴ Then a herald shouted out, "People of all races and nations and languages, listen to the king's command! ⁵ When you hear the sound of the horn, flute, zither, lyre, harp, pipes, and other musical instruments, bow to the ground to worship King Nebuchadnezzar's gold statue.⁶ *Anyone who refuses to obey will immediately be thrown into a blazing furnace."* Ouch! This Valley of Decision must have stung. Can you feel the bite of reality among the people? As our Truth # 3 declares, "Fiery Trials force you to choose sides." This leads you to the second half of the Truth: "Do you believe in God or will you yield to the idols of the World?" This Truth takes some Faith muscles to carry out. Why? As the stakes get higher, you will be forced to act on what you believe.

It is important to recognize that there are times when a *conclusion moment* is thrust upon you! You did not ask for it. You did not go looking for it. You did not wish it to come your way. It knocked on your heart's door without warning. No time to prepare. No time to call a prayer meeting. No time to sleep on it. Bam! It's in your face. What do you do? What would you do? Rach, Shach, and Benny were in this Valley, in a flash. I wonder what I would have done. I bet you do too. Could you look death in the eye with unflinching assurance as our young brothers did? Do you have their resolve to honor God in this manner? Such decisions are made years before the catastrophe arises. Brute strength does not get you through these decisions. Willpower does not hold a candle to this type of need. NO, these kinds of decisions are made while in the secret place of God's presence. Would you be willing to die for your faith in God? Be painfully honest? God already knows your heart. Has the God of the Universe so gripped your soul that without Him, life has no meaning, value, or purpose? I can assure you that when this kind of relationship exists, death has no mastery over you. How do I know this? Paul, the Apostle, shares such words as found in Philippians 1:20-24 (NIV), "20 For I fully expect and hope that I will never be ashamed, but that I will continue to be bold for Christ, as I have been in the past. And I trust that my life will bring honor to Christ, whether I live or die. 21 For to me, living means living for Christ, and dying is even better. 22 But if I live, I can do more fruitful work for Christ. So, I really don't know which is better. 23 I'm torn between two desires: I long to go and be with Christ, which would be far better for me. 24 But for your sakes, it is better that I continue to live."

"Dying is even better". Did I read that right? Yes. Torn between two desires? Unbelievable! The Apostle Paul welcomes death. He longs to be with his God in Heaven. He is ready to go! How can this be? Such poise he has in his pronouncement! What has the Apostle Paul found in his walk with Christ? Can we all have this same kind of relationship? Is it available today for the asking? What did he find? In a word: LOVE. Love motivates. Deep Love captivates. Paul was captivated with God's Love as found in Jesus Christ. His decision was YES because God had changed his life, inwardly. The Word of the Lord roars this profound truth as recorded by Paul in Romans 8:35-39 (NIV), "35 Can anything ever separate us from Christ's love? Does it mean He no longer loves us if we have trouble or calamity, or are persecuted, or hungry, or destitute, or in danger, or threatened with death? [36] (As the Scriptures say, "For your sake we are killed every day; we are being slaughtered like sheep.") [37] No, despite all these things, *overwhelming victory is ours through Christ, who* <u>loves</u> *us.*

[38] And I am convinced that nothing can ever separate us from God's love. Neither death nor life, neither angels nor demons, neither our fears for today nor our worries about tomorrow—not even the powers of hell can separate us from God's love. [39] No power in the sky above or in the earth below—*indeed, nothing in all creation will ever be able to separate us from the love of God that is revealed in Christ Jesus our Lord."*

For Shadrach, Meshach, and Abednego, this truth must have been the guiding star for their actions, too. They knew that death would not separate them from God so they were willing to embrace it. WOW! For the follower of Christ, you win, no matter what decisions could be today. Let's repeat the verse again in Joel 3:14 as we close:

"Multitudes, multitudes in the valley of decision! For the day of the LORD *is near in the valley of decision."*

You are there, too. Make WISE decisions, today!

As this chapter draws to a close, think through the last 30 days of the decisions in your life. Have they lead you closer to God and His purpose for your life? Has each decision brought you lasting love, joy, and peace? If not, the next 30 days of decisions can be game changers for you.

It's Your Move!

1. Do you agree that decisions shape your life? _____.
    How so? _____.
    _____.

2. Can you describe a time when trying to decide on a thing was
    extremely hard? _____.
    Why? _____.
    What did you learn about yourself? _____.
    _____.

3. What decisions are you avoiding today? _____.
    What actions should you take? _____.
    _____.

4. You make them...They Make You! What 3 decisions do you wish
    you had a "Do-Over"? a. _____
    _____ b. _____ c. _____
    _____. What does God want next? _____
    _____.

18

Are You Ready to Rumble?

Monday Night Raw. When I was working with high school students during my early ministry days back in the 1990's, we would often gather at my home to talk about life, love, and living for Jesus Christ. Occasionally, the students would convince me to tune into this wrestling program called *Monday Night Raw*. What a drama show that was! The high schoolers knew all the wrestlers and who was fighting whom. The statement made often was "Are you ready to rumble?"

When situations presented an opposing flare of any kind, one would yell "Are you ready to rumble? This would make us all laugh and helped to lighten the mood. We enjoyed our Monday nights together because the truth behind this slogan had some real grit associated with it. This primes us for Truth # 4:

4. *Fiery trials Bring out the Fight for what is right regardless if you will lose everything in the process.*

The word "*fight*" tends to always be displayed in light of the negative sense. I guess, most often, that is the case. However, there are times when fighting for what is right is merited and necessary. *The fight for righteousness must never lose its way in the storm of political correctness and cultural shifts.* Society celebrates the varied lifestyles today and pushes us for acceptance, tolerance, and equality. While loving the person is always at the heart of God's gospel, there is no wiggle room for ignoring God's standard for righteousness, holiness, and purity. Right is right and wrong is wrong, at any time and in any culture.

This was true in the days of our Hebrew friends, as well. At the core of living for God's truth, the formation of a gigantic statue would cause anyone to wonder about doing the right thing. The prideful King ordered this statue to be constructed in his honor as recorded in Daniel 3:1 (NIV), "**3** King Nebuchadnezzar made a gold statue ninety-feet tall and nine-feet wide and set it up on the plain of Dura in the province of Babylon." The golden image, some 9 stories tall, would be hard to overlook or ignore. At a time when idol worship was prevalent in the land, our young brothers knew the Word of the Lord as found in Exodus 20:1-6 (NKJV), "**2** "I *am* the LORD your God, who brought you out of the land of Egypt, out of the house of bondage. **3** "You shall have no other gods before Me. **4** "You shall not make for yourself a carved image—any likeness *of anything* that *is* in heaven above, or that *is* in the earth beneath, or that *is* in the water under the earth; **5** you shall not *bow down* to them nor serve them. For I, the LORD your God, *am* a jealous God, visiting the iniquity of the fathers upon the children to the third and fourth *generations* of those who hate Me, **6** *but showing mercy to thousands, to those who love Me and keep My commandments.*"

Clearly, obedience and reverence as well as a love for God was at the forefront of Shadrach, Meshach, and Abednego's minds. To live outside the realm of a heart surrendered to the God of their ancestors would be a breach of family loyalty as well as a dishonor upon their father's family. But, it went considerably deeper than that as it still does today. The first of the *Ten Commandments* as found in Exodus 20 gives a stern warning to thoughtless worship. The iniquity of the father's worship would be passed down to the great, great grandchildren. Four generations of suffering would be the result of foolish idolaters, bent on living without honoring the one true and living God. The other side of obedience and faithfulness to the God of the Bible was to bestow on one's family the Lord's mercy to a thousand generations. I don't exactly know how to compute that far down one's family tree, but what an inheritance to leave behind for your family.

Rach, Shach, and Benny knew the enormity of what was at stake. Bowing down to a false god was not an option, even if the King of the Land was demanding loyalty. Fiery trials cause the battle lines to be drawn. The King wanted them to cave. The brothers wanted to love and honor their God. A fight for righteousness was at-hand. When situations become tense, your resolve must be fixed and sure. In the heat of calamity, you must be sure of your response.

Are you ready to rumble? Seems like a silly slogan when you think about it. To Rumble! Have you ever used the word in a sentence? I don't recall any instance in recent years. The dictionary calls it a noun meaning:

a deep, heavy, somewhat muffled, continuous sound

In addition to a noun, it tags it with a verb tense for added usage:

to make a deep, heavy, somewhat muffled, continuous sound, as a thunder.

The God of Heaven rumbles (thunders) too as noted in Psalms 29:1-3 (NIV),

> "Ascribe to the LORD, you heavenly beings,
> ascribe to the LORD glory and strength.
> ² Ascribe to the LORD the glory due his name;
> worship the LORD in the splendor of his holiness.
> ³ The voice of the LORD is over the waters;
> the God of glory *thunders,*
> the LORD *thunders* over the mighty waters.

Why would the God of the universe thunder? Why would the God of *ALL* other gods rumble? Why would the Ancient of Days draw up battle lines for His people? In a word: *jealousy.* What? God jealous? No way! Why would God be jealous? *His name is jealous.* Look at the Scripture as found in Exodus 34:10-14 (NIV), "¹⁰ Then the LORD said: "I am making a covenant with you. Before all your people I will do wonders never before done in any nation in all the world. The people you live among will see how awesome is the work that I, the LORD, will do for you. ¹¹ *Obey what I command you today.* I will drive out before you the Amorites, Canaanites, Hittites, Perizzites, Hivites and Jebusites. ¹² Be careful not to make a treaty with those who live in the land where you are going, or they will be a snare among you.¹³ Break down their altars, smash their sacred stones and cut down their Asherah poles. ¹⁴ *Do not worship any other god,* for the LORD, *whose name is Jealous,* is a jealous God." In yet another place in the Bible, God is likened to a consuming fire, a jealous God. Check out the verse below to see it with your own eyes as found in Deuteronomy 4:24 (NIV), "²⁴ For the LORD your God *is* a consuming fire, *a jealous God.*"

Now, let's draw our minds back to the prideful King and the unsung heroes of the fiery furnace. It would be highly likely that Shadrach, Meshach, and Abednego *would* not bow to the golden statue out of their reverence for God, but, in truth, they *could* not bow their knee to the idol and worship it. They would be violating the first Commandment. *The grounded truths of their abiding faith welcomed <u>death over denial.</u>* When fighting for righteousness, you must decide what hill you are willing do die on. For Rach, Shach, and Benny, *they were willing to rumble (a slang word for a street fight) with death.*

The Bible has many places where God repeats himself concerning idols and the worship of them. One last instance is found in Deuteronomy 4:15-20 (NIV), "[15] You saw no form of any kind the day the LORD spoke to you at Horeb out of the fire. Therefore watch yourselves very carefully, [16] so that you do not become *corrupt* and make for yourselves an idol, an image of any shape, whether formed like a man or a woman, [17] or like any animal on earth or any bird that flies in the air, [18] or like any creature that moves along the ground or any fish in the waters below. [19] And when you look up to the sky and see the sun, the moon and the stars—*all the heavenly array*—do not be enticed into bowing down to them and worshiping things the LORD your God has apportioned to all the nations under heaven. [20] But as for you, the LORD took you and brought you out of the iron-smelting furnace, out of Egypt, to be the people of his inheritance, as you now are."

Let's take a few minutes and gnaw on this chapter a bit longer. Many of the above Scriptures proclaim God as Sovereign Ruler, Majestic King, Glorious Creator, and Thunderous Voice. He is so much *bigger* than our minds can fathom or comprehend. Is your soul thirsty? Do you long for peace with your Creator? Do you sense there is more to this life? Seek Him. Find Him. It's that simple. He loves you. His ways are not as ours nor are His thoughts as ours as noted in Isaiah 55:1-8 (NIV),

> "Come, all you who are thirsty,
> come to the waters;
> and you who have no money,

come, buy and eat!
Come, buy wine and milk
without money and without cost.
² Why spend money on what is not bread,
and your labor on what does not satisfy?
Listen, listen to me, and eat what is good,
and you will delight in the richest of fare.
³ Give ear and come to me;
listen, that you may live.
I will make an everlasting covenant with you,
my faithful love promised to David.
⁴ See, I have made him a witness to the peoples,
a ruler and commander of the peoples.
⁵ Surely you will summon nations you know not,
and nations you do not know will come running to you,
because of the LORD your God,
the Holy One of Israel,
for he has endowed you with splendor."
⁶ Seek the LORD while he may be found;
call on him while he is near.
⁷ Let the wicked forsake their ways
and the unrighteous their thoughts.
Let them turn to the LORD, and he will have mercy on them,
and to our God, for he will freely pardon.
⁸ *"For my thoughts are not your thoughts,*
neither are your ways my ways,"
declares the LORD.
"As the heavens are higher than the earth,
so are my ways higher than your ways
and my thoughts than your thoughts.

God is omniscient (all knowing), omnipresent (all places), and omnipotent (all powerful) *ALL* at the same time. Do you know this God? Do you walk daily with this God? He is jealous for you. He longs for you to know Him, personally. If you are sensing a tug on your heart to learn more about bowing your knee to the God who created you and fashioned an awesome plan for your life, go to the last chapter of the book to learn more about inviting Jesus Christ into your heart as Savior and Master (Lord). It will be the *best* decision you've ever made. You can count on it!

It's Your Move!

1. Do you care about righteous standards? _____.
    How so? _____.
    _____.

2. What have you fought for lately in a good way? _____. Why did
    it matter to you? _____.
    Did you consider your reputation? _____.
    _____.

3. What Truths are you willing to die for? _____.
    What actions prove this? _____.
    _____.

4. God is jealous over your life! How does that impact you? Be
    specific. What is your response? a. _____.
    _____ b. _____ c. _____
    _____. He wants a relationship with you. Do
    you want one with Him? Why or why not? _____.

19

Fear Factor

Have you ever been afraid? I mean really scared? I have. Let me lure you back to a time when my life was evolving from a struggling college student into an emerging young professional. The year was 1986 and I was 21-years old. As noted earlier, I was given a chance to enter a work-study program with big blue, IBM. The location was Boulder, Colorado. Scenic Rocky Mountains! Can you believe it? On the drive out to Boulder, I was traveling in a tiny VW Scirocco. I housed all my worldly possessions in an insignificant mini car. I was making the trip in a two-day run. Over 1400 miles from Atlanta, GA where I called home, at the time. So, my goal was roughly 700 miles of travel per day. As I was ramping down the first day travel demands, I stopped at a honky-tonk place somewhere in the middle of Kansas. It was late. It was dark. I was tired. I was fearful. I was a long way from the familiar. My eyes were always watchful around me. As I was making my way back to my car, after eating at this dive, I started to hear some wild sounds. It caught my attention, for sure. I started to run toward my car. When I got near my car, I downgraded my speed to a brisk walk. Then, I paused to look around. Out of no where, a stray cat jumps up on my left leg and held on for dear life. *I am not making this up!* Terror gripped my heart. I began to fear for my life. While I was shaking my leg to remove the cat, I was fumbling for my keys to unlock my car door. In the pitch black of night, I felt uneasy, afraid, and deeply concerned for my safety. I had never felt such terror before in my life. I was alone. Some 700 miles from home. No cell phones back then to call for a comforting word. Just me and Jesus. I finally got my car running and blazed out of the parking lot with wheels screaming. Back on to the interstate I went. It took what seemed like hours to return to a normal breathing rate, unclutter my mind of the danger, and know that everything would be fine. Now, some 30 years later, that imagery still reminds me of what *real* fright looks like. *It's ugly. It's unrelenting. It's paralyzing. It's hurtful.*

In our society today, we make a spectacle of fear. We look it in the eyes and say, "I dare you!" To showcase this truth, consider the reality TV show, called *"Fear Factor"*. It aired on NBC from 2001 to 2006. The 5-year run of the show featured contestants battling for money, fame, and bragging rights as to who had the most guts to overcome their *biggest* fears. I must confess that I watched the show every week in awe and asked myself the question if I could do what these contestants were doing. Most of the time, it would be <u>never</u>. Crazy stuff was displayed each week such as eating cockroaches, getting bit by a snake, almost drowning, being buried in spiders, jumping off a high building, etc. It messed with one's heart, mind, emotion, and body. If I were honest, the show intrigued me. Why? How could one person be so brave while another be so afraid? What did he or she have over another contestant? How did one's upbring create self-assurance while another's generated cowardliness?

Interestingly enough, the variety of fears among the people was also mesmerizing. Some fears taunted the physical. Some fears bullied the emotional. Some fears stalked the mental. _All_ fears pushed the envelope of strength, courage, and confidence. What would possess a person to be on the show in the first place? Have we no modesty in dealing with life's quiet, inward battles? Well for sure, these contestants were willing to put their struggles on public display for the weekly viewing audience.

As we reflect on our Jewish brothers, once again. They were in a prehistoric _"Fear Factor"_. This "Fear of all fears" was confronting death and the here-after. Of all the fears known to mankind, the idea of dying is among the top fears, if not the Number I. Death messes with the mind, heart, and emotion. Its rudeness is _real_. It looms in every hospice room. Its sinister laugh can be heard at funerals. It causes deep emotional loss and grieving for the surviving family members. It marks you, deeply. It really does! Yet, for the Christ follower, death is a defeated foe as journaled in I Corinthians 15:53 – 57, (NIV), "53 For the perishable must clothe itself with the imperishable, and the mortal with immortality. 54 When the perishable has been clothed with the imperishable, and the mortal with immortality, then the saying that is written will come true: _"Death has been swallowed up in victory."_

55 "Where, O death, is your victory?
Where, O death, is your sting?"

56 The sting of death is sin, and the power of sin is the law. 57 But _thanks be to God! He gives us the victory through our Lord Jesus Christ._

The above declaration must have been resident in the hearts of Shadrach, Meshach, and Abednego. This leads us to the Number 5 Truth:

5. *Fiery trials do not cause* <u>*FEAR*</u> *or* <u>*INTIMIDATION*</u> *for the "SECURE" Christian.*

There was not an *ounce* of hesitation when the King of Babylon gave them the ultimate choice: bow or die? This fear factor moment was a nail biter as the wondering crowd peered on in astonishment. What they were unwilling to do, Rach, Shach, and Benny did gladly. They kissed death's cheek and said "Bring it on!" No intimidation. No second thoughts. No bargaining table edicts. *Bold, Brash, and Believable.* Secure followers of Jesus Christ are relaxed at such times. How is that possible, you may wonder? Many do! The easy answer can be found in 2 Corinthians 4:18 (NIV), "[18] So we fix our eyes not on what is seen, but on what is unseen, since what is seen is temporary, but what is unseen is eternal."

Where do you fix your eyes? Do you peek at life through temporal lenses? Fixated on the here and now? Only concerned with what you see around you? Be honest, now! It's easy to do, yet, the outcome is worry, anxiety, and panic. The unseen world is *more* real than the seen world. If you know the Lord, you are a citizen of heaven and will one day return to your proper homeland. You are only passing through Earth as mentioned in John 14:1-3 (NIV), "Do not let your hearts be troubled. You believe in God; believe also in me. [2] My Father's house has many rooms; if that were not so, would I have told you that I am going there to prepare a place for you?[3] *And if I go and prepare a place for you, I will come back and take you to be with me that you also may be where I am.*"

I am looking forward to the day when Jesus Christ comes back for His Bride, the local Church. Why? I'll tell you my *"own"* opinion. Don't feel you must adopt my thoughts. I don't know about you, but the world is becoming more of a strange place, every day. In the United States of America, in 2019, so much unrest is happening. The racial progress of years gone by is unraveling before our eyes. Fighting in the streets is common today among groups that hate each other. It's on the nightly news. You can't escape it.

The moral decay of sexual understanding is running wild. In America today, the notion of male, female, and "I'm unsure" is prevalent. It is just my opinion, but the ultimate offense to a Holy God, one's Creator, is that when you were born, you declare He messed up with your gender. Such arrogance is unmerited.

In addition to gender identity is the idea of sexual orientation. Marriage is <u>nowadays</u> legal between men with men as well as woman with woman. The traditional view of family is under attack in our modern times. Many now say "What God originally started in the Garden of Eden with Adam and Eve is outdated and narrow-minded!" Intolerant is what the world is now calling the committed, follower of Christ who adheres to the Living, Abiding Word of God.

Next, consider sexual purity as well. In the news as of late is the tidal wave of women coming forward who were sexually abused by political figures, Hollywood producers, Coaches, TV Anchors and other prominent people. The daily news continues to add to this mound of broken women, hurt by people they trusted with their female soul. *Shameful!*

If this were not enough, consider the mass shootings of our times. We watch the news in horror as reports of these shootings unfold. Concert goers gunned down at night. *Cowardly!* Church attenders shot at point blank ranges, including young children. *Diabolic!* Movie theaters and elementary schools were once safe venues to attend. *No longer!* Shopping malls? Maybe. Football stadiums? Not in this present day. Is there a safe place any longer? *Alarm has gripped our society in this contemporary era and has paralyzed our emotions.*

<u>*Jesus come quickly!*</u> *You would do well to fix your eyes on a Heavenly gaze.* This world is not our final stop along Eternity's time line. We're going home. That is our hope. That is our comfort. That is our peace.

Fear does not have to intimidate you as a child of God. The Word of God makes <u>no</u> mistakes about the final outcome. We Win.

Could it be that the Babylon times were so messed up for Shadrach, Meshach, and Abednego that death would have been a welcomed escape? Could the King have life so unbalanced, unpredictable, and unhealthy that one's heart walked with uncertainty? Whatever the state of affairs, these boys were willing to embrace death with confidence, courage, and candor. You can too! Jesus Christ gave Mary and Martha powerful words to tuck back in their minds as recorded in John 11:25 (NIV), "²⁵ Jesus said to her, "I am the resurrection and the life. The one who believes in me will live, even though they die; ²⁶ and whoever lives by believing in me will never die. *Do you believe this?*"

Never Die? Grasp that truth! Yes, your body will revisit the ground. Yes, a funeral will take place. *However,* your spirit will <u>never</u> die as a Believer in Jesus Christ. You will live forever with the Lord as a child of the Living God. Death's sting has lost its stinger. Jesus has broken death's hold. Can I share one more Scripture with you as we close this chapter? It should give us the ultimate reason to tell fear to "Back off". You see it at football games. You see it on signs held by street evangelists. You saw it painted on Tim Tebow's face as a college quarterback. That's right: John 3:16. Look at each word in this compelling verse:

"¹⁶ For God <u>so loved</u> the world that he gave his one and only Son, that whoever believes in him shall not perish but have eternal life."

The *Fear Factor life* has been canceled. No more new shows. No more reruns on TV land. Canceled. Canceled. Canceled. Let that sink into your soul. Fear is no longer a factor. We Win. You Win too… If you are in Christ! Why?

¹⁷ For God did not send his Son into the world to condemn the world, <u>but to save the world through him</u>.

You were worth saving! Jesus was your Rescuer. No longer condemned. Rather, saved. That is the ultimate story line in all of human history. These two verses in the Holy Scriptures tell why the Fear Factor life can't exist in the heart of a Christ Follower. We are Saved! Now, that is Good news. Let's move forward to Chapter 20. We are in the home stretch. Thanks for hanging in there.

It's Your Move!

I. Have you ever been really scared? _____.

What did you do? _____.

_____.

2. Fear Factor! Do you remember the show? _____.

Did you watch it? _____. Why or why not? _____

_____.

What did you learn about yourself? _____.

_____.

3. What fears to you nurse today? _____.

_____. (Be honest!) Which ones need broken by

God's power? _____.

4. Are you afraid to die? Why? or why not? _____

_____ Jesus defeated death on the Cross, do you

believe this? _____.

Would you like to know Jesus, personally? _____.

Why not pause now and give your heart and life to Christ.

20

Being Consumed or Being Conformed

Do you try to fit in? Blend into the crowd? Merge into the fabric of uniformity? There is no humiliation in doing so, but the <u>best</u> life offered is <u>not</u> "going with the flow". *You were made for more.* So, enjoy it! An often-celebrated set of verses from the Bible can be found in Romans 12:1-2 (NIV), "**12** Therefore, I urge you, brothers and sisters, *in view of God's mercy,* to <u>offer</u> your bodies as a living sacrifice, holy and pleasing to God—this is your true and proper worship. ² Do not <u>conform</u> to the pattern of this world, but be <u>transformed</u> by the *renewing* of your mind. Then you will be able to test and approve what God's will is—*his good, pleasing and perfect will.*"

You get these verses quoted quite often in local church services. They might even be considered "famous" verses. Not famous in a vain way, rather famous in a highly used way. Why? The *big* ask from these verses puts you in the driver's seat to decide. They are not demanding anything of you, but suggesting an action based on a fact, A *big action, nonetheless.* However, the asking lens to peer through is a defined one:

in view of God's mercy. Asking to lay down one's life might be an over-the-top request in any other context. But, not this one. Yes, you could walk away if your uncle Frank, the crazy one at all the Christmas gatherings, wanted you to give up this precious commodity called *Life.* What about cousin, Mary Gail, cute as a June bug, asking you to give up the ghost just this one time? Or, in the final analysis, maybe offering up a spare kidney to your best friend, Sticks, would be acceptable, *but not death.* Nevertheless, this verse is asking for a Living Sacrifice commitment. How is that possible? The viewing lens makes all the difference: *In view of God's mercy!*

The Apostle Paul sets the stage for the *big* ask from God, but he makes sure that you know the lattice to peer through: *In view of God's mercy. You see it changes everything about your life.* Stop for a minute and consider these five words. Is God merciful? Yes. Has He been merciful to you? Yes. Has He been merciful to you, today? Yes. How do we know? The Bible gives the concluding verdict as described in Lamentations 3:22-23 (NLT),

> "The faithful love of the LORD never ends!
> *His mercies never cease.*
> 23 Great is his faithfulness;
> *his mercies begin afresh each morning.*

Did you latch on to those two italicized sentences? The first one, "His mercies never cease." They are a constant just like the sun rising each morning. Just like the ocean waves crashing each day. Just like breathing in the richness of clean air into your lungs. They are unending! That can't be overlooked with a casual glance. In life, everything has a limit. Money runs out. Patience runs out. Health runs out. Careers run out. In contrast, God's mercy never ceases. We don't often use the word *never* in sentences because of its bold claim. However, God can! And, He does. He uses it for a great need of ours: mercy. Thank Him that He has a limitless supply. Available and awaiting as your eyes open each morning. Tap into it. Extinguish its full contents each day, if you can. Tomorrow has a renewed supply coming. We serve an unlimited God.

Secondly, "His mercies begin afresh each morning." Wow! With each new dawn comes a mountain of newfangled mercies. Powerful, truthful, and necessary. We need it. Just like the need for love, we have a *huge* need for mercy: God's mercy! So, in light of the volume and frequency of His mercies, now the big ask can happen. In view of God's mercy, offer your bodies as a *Living Sacrifice*. It seems reasonable based on the particulars. In fact, the above Scripture calls this action true and proper. It is an act of worship toward a God who is merciful toward you on a moment-by-moment basis.

In view of God's mercy, then the next big ask comes: *"Don't live like the world."* Stop conforming to its thinking, values, purposes, and pleasures. The Bible calls it a *pattern*. Have you ever made a garment from scratch? Have you ever seen one being made? It uses what is called a *pattern*. An outline of the shapes is used to construct the final dress, shirt, or pants. The pattern determines the *shape*. The patterns of this world will determine what *shape* your life ends up like, if you conform to it. Be different. Live different. Do it for God, in view of His mercy.

Lastly, *"Be transformed!"* How? By the *renewing* of your mind. Change your thinking by allowing God's Word to wash your brain. Notice, I didn't say "Get brain washed." The world thinks that of Christianity. Mindless surrender to a set of rules and code of ethics. No, I said to launder your brain. A few synonyms for the word renew are to *renovate* or *refurbish*. I like those terms as well. It means to create an updated objective for an existing object. Bathe your brain, daily, with God's purifying Word. Out with the old. In with the new. At this time, let's introduce our Number 6 Truth:

6. *Fiery trials <u>CONSUME</u> the unbeliever, yet <u>CONFORMS</u> the Believer.*

Not, conformity in the general sense, going along with everyone else in the multitudes. No, this conformity is to a person: Jesus Christ. God's chief aim for your life is for you to be like Jesus. Fiery trials bring us to a place were the heat-of-life make us moldable and yielded to God. *Therefore, Life's pain makes us change.* I think that is why God is always allowing us to be put in difficult situations. While we don't welcome it, we need its effect. We are a stubborn people bent on our own direction. God has to get our attention. Discomfort does that! To become like Jesus is God's goal line as found in Romans 8:28-29 (NIV), "28 And we know that in all things God works for the good of those who love him, who have been called according to his purpose. 29 For those God foreknew he also predestined to be *conformed to the image of his Son*, that he might be the firstborn among many brothers and sisters."

Becoming like Jesus involves one key word: *surrender*. To die to one's self is hard. It really is. *I'm just being transparent here.* It is for all of us. *Surrender is a curse word in our society, today.* Nobody wants to give up the drive to act freely. It shows weakness and meekness, so we think. On the other hand, the fact remains, *surrender is your pathway to blessing and Eternal glory.* Dying to one's will is not normal. It never is! The supernatural kicks in when the will is <u>submitted</u> to God's directives. That is why the conclusion of our Romans 12:2b is so profound, "Then you will be able to test and approve what God's will is—*his good, pleasing and perfect will.*" When you get your will out of the way, you are open to God's will for your life...*his good, pleasing, and perfect will.*

As we reflect back on the story of the Fiery Furnace, a parody exists. Watch this: "22 The king's command was so urgent and the furnace *so hot that the flames of the fire <u>killed</u> the soldiers who took up Shadrach, Meshach and Abednego*," Consumed in the line of duty! A human torch. *How can the flames kill one person (the King's court) and not another? (Rach, Shach, and Benny).* Good Question. How can the unexpected death of a child destroy one family and yet draw another family closer together? How can a medical report cripple one's faith in God while another person seeks God with earnestness? How can the divorce extinguish the abuser's life, but bring comfort to the abused person now living free and in safety? Flames abound in the spectacles of every day life. We *all* face them. Some crumble under the weight of them. Some use them as stepping stones to a greater life and richer purpose. What consumes one will conform another. It is a paradox of epic proportion. God uses parody! It serves Him well.

Could it be that Shadrach, Meshach, and Abednego saw everything "in view of God's mercy"? What if they were aware of God's chief aim: To be made like Him? Would it be true and proper to give one's life for the Creator of it? Rach, Shach, and Benny thought so. *The Great Exchange:* Giving up what you can not keep to gain what you can not lose! Let it go. Loosen your grip on life's to-do list. Walk away from the pressure to be busy. In dying, you win. In surrender, you are at liberty. In the interchange, life's aroma surrounds us with beauty and hope, once again. To offer your life is wise. To live a life conformed to Christ is worth it all. Lay it down for Him. You'll find it renewed, renovated, and refurbished. Check out this last verse for this chapter. It meant so much to me be back in 1986. After years of alcohol and drug abuse during my adolescent years, I needed its truth for my life in my early twenties. Here it is as chronicled in, 2 Corinthians 5: 17 (NIV),

"17 Therefore, if anyone is in Christ, the new creation has come: The old has gone, the new is here!

A brand-new shiny life awaited me. I took the offer! I needed the promise. In Christ; the old left me. In Christ; the new found me. Now, over 30 years later, I still have it. A brand-new shiny life awaits you! That is, if you want it. A brand-new shiny life. Why? His mercies never cease. Why? His mercies begin afresh each morning. What could be better than that? Absolutely nothing!

It's Your Move!

I. Consumed or Conformed. Do you get to choose your outcome?
_____. How do you know?

_____.

What have you decided? _____.

2. In view of God's Mercy! Your initial thought? _____.
_____. Do you need His mercy today?

Why? _____.

3. Patterns create shapes. What shape is your life in?

_____.

What two things would you like to change today? _____

_____.

4. *Bathe your brain.* In what ways is your thinking now hurting your
life? _____.

God wants to "*renew*" your mind. What steps can you begin to
implement? a. _____ b. _____

_____ c._____.

21

Finding Freedom in the Furnace

Freedom. It's a controversial word. Always has been. Probably, always will be. Blood was shed to gain it. Hundreds of years of US history note that fact. Young soldiers, drafted to defend it, coming home in boxes from foreign lands. *Blood is still being shed to keep it.* This time it is called terrorism. 911 used to call to memory the phone number need for emergencies. Today, 911 represents a dual meaning. On September 11th (9/11), 2001, our nation watched in horror as the Twin Towers in New York City came crashing down killing countless thousands of innocent people whose only crime that day was being faithful to their employer. Simply acting on a conviction to provide for one's family by being a dedicated employee, they found themselves in the center of a bad dream. It was real, though. Very real! Families were forever changed that day. Our Nation was forever changed that day. Your freedom was forever changed that day. No, freedom is certainly not free. And, freedom is not cheap. It costs something to receive it. Remember, it always costs blood.

Let's dig back into history (His Story) a bit further. Spiritual freedom. Do you have it? Do you need it? Do you even want it? *Blood was shed to gain it, too.* Not just any blood would work for this procurement. The sticker price was too high for human blood to work. It required exorbitant blood as noted in 1 Peter 1:17-21 (NIV), "[17] Since you call on a Father who judges each person's work impartially, live out your time as foreigners here in reverent fear. [18] For you know that it was not with perishable things such as silver or gold that you were <u>redeemed</u> from the empty way of life handed down to you from your ancestors, [19] *but with the precious blood of Christ, a lamb without blemish or defect.* [20] He was chosen before the creation of the world, but was revealed in these last times for your sake. [21] Through him you believe in God, *who raised him from the dead and glorified him,* and so your faith and hope are in God."

Precious blood was the rate of exchange for this acquisition. *God saw you as that valuable.* He gave a priceless gift to us, the blood of His own son, Jesus Christ, on the Cross. We could not earn it. We did not deserve it. However, God sees us through the lens of grace. I purposely underlined the word redeemed above. It means to discharge or fulfill as in a pledge or promise. Think of it this way. You and I owed a debt that we were not able to pay. The debt of sin puts us in a place of slavery to the owner, Satan. He held the deed to your life with your name written in plain view for all to see. This burden was real, heavy, and forever. You had no hope of settling this debt. You were doomed. Why? Sin separates.

The *Roman Road* was something I was taught in my early walk with God as it gives a quick summary to show our true state of need:

1. *We Fell*
   - Romans 3:23 (NIV), "[23] for all have sinned and fall short of the glory of God,"

2. *We Deserve*
   - Romans 6:23, (NIV) "²³ For the wages of sin is death, but the gift of God is eternal life in Christ Jesus our Lord."

3. *We Believe*
   - Romans 5:8 (NIV), "⁸ But God demonstrates his own love for us in this: While we were still sinners, Christ died for us."

4. *We Receive*
   - Romans 10:9-10 (NIV), "⁹ If you declare with your mouth, "Jesus is Lord," and believe in your heart that God raised him from the dead, you will be saved. ¹⁰ For it is with your heart that you believe and are justified, and it is with your mouth that you profess your faith and are saved."

We were prisoners to sin as the above verses noted. Yet, God demonstrated His love for us in such a profound way. He loved us in spite of our condition. He gave His son, Jesus, to redeem us from the debt. As the dictionary noted, Jesus fulfilled the pledge and thus discharged us from the responsibility to keep making payments. *Only God loves you that much.*

Do you feel like you are bound up today? Do negative thoughts hinder your life? Do you live in a state of worry and fear for what tomorrow holds? Do you wonder about the after-life? Does total freedom sound like a pipe dream? This leads us to our Next Truth, No. 7:

7. *Fiery trials <u>BURN UP</u> the bands the <u>WORLD</u> places upon you.*

Let's go back to Shadrach, Meshach, and Abednego and recall their freedom story. For emphasis, I want to have you read these verses again found in Daniel 3:21-23 (NIV), ²¹ So these men, wearing their robes, trousers, turbans and other clothes, were *bound* and thrown into the blazing furnace. [22] The king's command was so urgent and the furnace so hot that the flames of the fire <u>killed</u> the soldiers who took up Shadrach, Meshach and Abednego, [23] and these three men, *firmly tied,* fell into the blazing furnace."

Bound and firmly tied could describe the state of many lives today. We live out our daily existence bound-up with regret, remorse, and resistance. We want to move forward with hope, promise, and destiny, but we feel stuck in our present condition.

Firmly tied is recorded in the story of our Babylon brothers. The King didn't just want to make sure they were tied, but firmly tied. There is a difference. If you were just tied, you might find a way of escape. Like a magician who can get out of a trunk or a strait jacket, there is a glimmer of hope for the performer. Conversely, *when you are firmly tied, every possibility of freedom is gone.* You are subject to a trajectory that leads you off of life's best path. This leads to hopelessness and despair.

In heroic fashion, the bound and firmly tied brothers dumbfound the prideful King. This is where the God of Abraham, Isaac, and Jacob showed up in a big way. *He will in your life, as well.* The King, feeling pretty sure of himself, gets an eyeful as cited in Daniel 3:24-25 (NIV), "[24] Then King Nebuchadnezzar *leaped* to his feet in *amazement* and asked his advisers, "Weren't there three men that <u>we</u> *tied* up and threw into the fire?"

They replied, "Certainly, Your Majesty."

[25] He said, "Look! I see four men *walking around* in the fire, <u>unbound,</u> and <u>unharmed,</u> and the fourth looks like a son of the gods."

I want to include verse 25 once again in another translation, the King James Version (KJV) as it paints a very clear picture, "[25] He answered and said, Lo, I see four men loose, walking in the midst of the fire, *and they have no hurt*; and the form of the fourth is like *the Son of God.*

My Dear Friend, could you believe in such a miracle? Would your heart wrap around the fact that three men went into a flaming furnace, seven times hotter than normal. The heat of the inferno was enough to kill the soldiers as they threw Rach, Shach, and Benny into the fire, but our Hebrew heroes were free, unharmed, and walking around in the flames. And, they were joined by a fourth, *Honorary Guest, the Son of God. (Jesus Christ).*

The fiery trials you face on a daily basis don't have to leave you flattened, without hope of recovery. God has the ability to take you from a bound and firmly tied state to an unbound and unharmed state. You don't have to escape the fiery trials of life because they are used by God to burn up the bands the world places on you. How can they be walking around in the midst of the fire? God! How can they be free from the bands? God! How can they be unharmed? God! How can they be with the Son of God? Good Question. That will be explored in the next chapter. However, let's apply what we've learned here.

Do you feel bound up and firmly tied in any area of your life? Have you tried to get free on your own, only to get stuck once again? Do you feel you have given up trying to walk in freedom in any area of your life? Be honest here. There is freedom in Jesus Christ. This is echoed in John 8:36 (NIV)," So if the Son sets you *free*, you will be *free indeed."* Do you long to be free indeed? *The answer is found in the source of our spiritual freedom.* When life hits you hard, you can have the Son of God walking with you in the blazing furnace. He will, you know! *He's waiting for you to invite Him.*

It's Your Move!

1. Freedom is not free! What does that mean to you?
   Why so? _____.
   _____.

2. Where were you when 9/11 happened? _____.
   How did it impact you? _____.
   Do you live in fear of terrorism? _____.
   _____.

3. Do you feel bound up today in any area? _____.
   What would it take to be free? _____.
   What have you tried in the past? _____.

4. Jesus Christ can set you free from sin. Have you settled your
   spiritual freedom with Him? _____.
   How would it feel to be "free indeed"? _____
   _____. Is Jesus knocking on
   your heart right now? Why not invite Him into your life!
   Walking in freedom is possible with Jesus by your side.

22

Knocking on Opportunities Door

I love the word *opportunity*. I guess that is because I am entrepreneurial by nature. I enjoy developing things from scratch. I relish the dreaming stage, the planning stage, the implementation stage, the production stage, and the final stage. The design engineering world calls the concept of stages, "cradle-to-grave". Yes, opportunity is out there!

Deep down, we all yearn for a good opportunity to present itself. A lady holds her breath during the moment of a proposal. The man gets butterflies at the word of a new promotion. The rising college student paces with excitement while holding the acceptance letter in hand. The expecting parents walk back and forth awaiting the news of the baby's gender not to mention the pending arrival. What about the notion of moving to a retirement location, long planned for by the aging couple? Why? In a word: opportunity.

Opportunity delivers change. Change births faith. Faith supplies hope. Hope is the oxygen of the soul. You would do well to memorize this little flow of words. Mathematically, we would conclude that opportunity produces hope with a series of ingredients moving in between. Hope is the icing on top of your proverbial cake called *Life*. Without hope, your life is unbearable. Yet, the with introduction of opportunity, *Hope* is waiting to make its arrival.

This leads us to Truth No. 8 about Fiery Trials:

8.   *Fiery trials give Jesus Christ the <u>OPPORTUNITY</u> to <u>JOIN</u> you in the fire.*

No one would have ever believed, certainly not the King of Babylon, that Shadrach, Meshach, and Abednego, would graciously agree to take death as an option. Who does that kind of thing, anyway? Yet, grounded by their faith in the Lord, they confronted their fears and defied the mandate to worship the Golden statue even when death was awaiting them. I don't know about your thoughts, but these guys were *gutsy*. What was the reason for their steadfast courage?

Truth No. 8 is the reason for their brashness. When life turns upside down, do you have such confidence? We should! Jesus Christ joins us when life sucker punches us in the gut. He is there when the doctors deliver the cancer report. He is there when the aging spouse is asked to unplug the life supports. Jesus is present when a divorce decree is final. He is with you when the miscarriage arises as you try to start a new family. Jesus walks the halls of the lonely college student away from home for the first time. He sleeps in the bed beside the young child who is convinced the boogie man is hiding in the closet. No stranger to pain, Jesus is in the hospice room as the lurking, death angel comes calling for his next participant. Get that down in your DNA. *God is with you, always.* He promises such. This fact is echoed throughout the Scriptures as found in Deuteronomy 31:6 (NIV), "Be strong and courageous. Do not be afraid or terrified because of them, for the LORD *your* God goes with *you; he will never leave you nor forsake you."*

Again, in Joshua 1:5 (NIV), "No one will be able to stand against *you* all the days of *your* life. As I was with Moses, so I will be with you; *I will never leave you nor forsake you."*

Next, as recorded in Psalms 9:10 (NIV), "Those who know your name trust in you, for you, LORD, *have never forsaken those who seek you.*"

Finally, in Hebrews 3:5 (NIV), "Keep your lives free from the love of money and be content with what you have, *because God has said, "Never will I leave you; never will I forsake you."*

One of the most comforting Scriptures can be found in Daniel 3:25 (KJV) as noted earlier, "²⁵ He answered and said, Lo, I see four men loose, walking in the midst of the fire, and they have no hurt; and the form of the fourth is *like the Son of God.*" We learned in the previous chapter that they were unbound and unharmed. While that is great news, how would it feel and look if Rach, Shach, and Benny were completely alone in the Fiery Flames? Horrifying, probably! No, when you stand up for God, He will stand up for you by joining you in the midst of your combat. You are never alone. If the above four verses were not enough, this theme is repeated from Genesis to Revelation. God is "In" us. God is "With" us. and, God is "For" us. In the blazing furnaces of life, Jesus Christ is standing toe-to-toe with you. You are not running solo. You never have to battle alone. In any and every circumstance where life finds you, *He finds you!* Now, that is *awesome* news.

Shadrach, Meshach, and Abednego helped the King to eat some humble pie, at least he is eating his words as recorded in Daniel 3:15 (NIV), "¹⁵ Now when you hear the sound of the horn, flute, zither, lyre, harp, pipe and all kinds of music, if you are ready to fall down and worship the image I made, very good. But if you do not worship it, you will be thrown immediately into a blazing furnace. *Then what god will be able to rescue you from my hand?"*

Kings never expect to be wrong. Certainly, not this one. He leaped to his feet in disbelief. I'm sure he had summoned others to the jaws of death in the fiery furnace. Nothing new there. Could it be that the King got too smug and sure of his own efforts? Yet, opportunity has a way of showing up for a magnificent show. The King got to see this first hand: Opportunity delivers change. Change births faith. Faith supplies hope. *Hope is the oxygen of the soul.*

Dear Friend, fiery trials are not evil. Fiery trials are not punishment for sins committed. Fiery trials are not God's way of cornering you into to willful submission. Fiery trials give Jesus Christ an opportunity to join you in the midst of the flames. He is there for your comfort. He is there for your security. He is there for your peace of mind. He is there for your protection. He is there for your hope. God is there!

In a swansong word as I close this chapter, this last verse should be of great comfort as registered in Psalms 37:35 (NIV), "I was young and now I am old, yet I have never seen the righteous *forsaken* or their children begging bread." Whether in emotional or mental need. God's is there. Whether in physical provision. God is present. Whether in relational healing, God is with you. Whether in spiritual pruning, God sees you. And, He joins you there! Don't panic. Praise Him. Don't worry. Worship Him. Hallelujah. This next Chapter brings wind to your sails. God celebrates when His children honor Him in trying times. Let's take a look.

It's Your Move!

1. Opportunity is everywhere. Do you agree? _____.
   Do you look for it? _____.
   In what ways? _____.

2. *Opportunity delivers change. Change births faith. Faith supplies hope.* What
   does this speak to you? _____.
   Why or why not? _____
   _____.

3. Why is "Hope oxygen for the soul"? _____.
   _____.

4. When life goes sideways, do you think God leaves you to figure
   it out on your own? _____
   _____.

5. Do you find Jesus is with you during times of testing? Why or
   why not? _____.

23

Operating at the Next Level

Don't you love it when someone is singing a new tune because of a realization of something learned. Newfangled information generates novel awareness. Fresh mindfulness produces a different belief system to anchor to. In an instant, the way we see things can be overhauled. This could not have been truer for the King of Babylon. He had to take his foot out of his mouth and recognize that he was *wrong*. Just know this, the tide turns for your favor if you honor God. This final confrontation is recorded in Daniel 3:26-30 (NIV),

"[26] Nebuchadnezzar then approached the opening of the blazing furnace and shouted, "Shadrach, Meshach and Abednego, *servants of the Most High God, come out! Come here!*"

So, Shadrach, Meshach and Abednego came out of the fire, [27] and the satraps, prefects, governors and royal advisers *crowded around them.* They saw that the fire had not harmed their bodies, nor was a hair of their heads singed; their robes were not scorched, *and there was no smell of fire on them.*

^{28} Then Nebuchadnezzar said, *"Praise be to the God of Shadrach, Meshach and Abednego, who has sent his angel and rescued his servants! They trusted in him and defied the king's command and were willing to give up their lives rather than serve or worship any god except their own God.* ^{29} Therefore I <u>decree</u> that the people of any nation or language who say anything against the God of Shadrach, Meshach and Abednego be cut into pieces and their houses be turned into piles of rubble, for *no other god can save in this way."*

^{30} *Then the king <u>promoted</u> Shadrach, Meshach and Abednego in the province of Babylon.*

The final Truth, No. 9 of Fiery Trials is based on Daniel 3:30:

9. *Fiery trials produce* <u>**CHARACTER**</u> *conducive for* <u>**PROMOTION**</u>.

This outcome is remarkable. It's a miracle of epic proportions. Not only did the three Jewish brothers live through the fiery ordeal, but in the end, *they got promoted to a higher level of service for the King.* What! How could this be? Staying true to God, in the midst of challenging tribulations, generates a character that is attractive, compelling, and rare. *You shine brightly during times like these.* People take notice! God is glorified when you weather tough times. Nevertheless, your character is developed to heights of honor and usefulness. It is amazing to watch this principle at work. It was working in Moses' life. It was operational in Joseph's life. It was present in the life of King David. These ingredients were on display for the Apostle Paul (a former killer) as he recorded most of the New Testament from a prison cell. Wow! God does not waste an occasion in your world to take you to the next level. I like to call it promote-ability. I know that is not a word in our modern language, but it works well here. *You grow in your ability to be promoted during perplexing life moments.* Don't dismiss this. The dictionary shares this meaning about promote: *To advance in rank, dignity or position.* That sums it up. Life is about moving you forward, onward, and upward. No coasting to the finish line. It's too exquisite to waste in taking the easy way out.

See fiery trials with _new_ eyes. Your elevation is waiting. In the loneliness of the moment, the pain is ferocious. _I get that._ Yet, God is setting you up for advancement, upgrading your dignity as you travel on toward a new position. Sweet, isn't it? Who would have believed our Brothers Band, RSB, would be living the dream in Babylon? Its sure beats being a human torch.

Notice a divine, dual _win_ in the story. While Shadrach, Meshach, and Abednego got their earthly promotion. Guess who else got promoted: _God._ Yes! _God did._ The other meaning of promote is as follows: to make more known. Advertisers do it. We accept that. Sports teams do it. We want that. We advertise our wedding plans to friends and family. Promotion has always been around.

The King got a revelation about Jehovah - God. He is the God who saves. The King's responsiveness is quite different now as penned in Daniel 3:28 (NIV), "²⁸ Then Nebuchadnezzar said, _"Praise be to the God of Shadrach, Meshach and Abednego, who has sent his angel and rescued his servants! They trusted in him and defied the king's command and were willing to give up their lives rather than serve or worship any god except their own God."_ God became more known. Yes, the once foolish King, numb to a Higher Power, now saw the Highest Power, the God of _All_ Glory, deployed on behalf of His own children. The King was confronted with a loyalty of Faith to a God who IS. The Great I AM of Eternity, the Rock of Ages, the Father of Creation, and the Seed of the Woman showed up and showed out in the Fiery Furnace. The King of Babylon had a front row seat to this larger-than-life encounter. Worldly, in context, the King saw something he had never seen before. God, Himself!

It moved the King's heart. It had to. He was pronouncing the oracles of God to the crowd of onlookers. It sure got his attention in the moment. This is evident in his next verbiage as listed in Daniel 3:29 (NIV), "²⁹ Therefore I _decree_ that the people of any nation or language who say _anything_ against the God of Shadrach, Meshach and Abednego be cut into pieces and their houses be turned into piles of rubble, *for no other god can save in this way."* Think with me for a minute. Could the King have given mental assent to his gods or even his 90-feet tall by 9-feet wide golden image of himself, if he knew a true God existed? Would any of these gods show up to save a human life in a very real fiery furnace? If they were willing to show up, could they do anything about the dilemma at-hand? Probably not. I believe the King was at an intellectual crossroads. He had never seen Deity up close and personal before. False gods? Every day of his reign. Deity? Not up to this point. If he had, he would have discharged building his golden statue or thoughtlessly forcing others to worship it. The King of Babylon was spiritually marked that day. Forever tattooed in his mind and etched on his heart.

His actions gave the confirmation to the divine meeting. He wanted men working for him with such bold convictions as to live without thought for life and limb. Men who were fully devoted to their beliefs that surrender to a worldly mantra was not an option. Men who could look the King in the eye and say *"No"* to his commands. These were not *"Yes"* men and that was eye-catching to the King of Babylon.

Promotion came. Unexpected. Yes. Unearned. Never. *God is the Author of Promotion.* He orchestrates our life's events in such a manner as to fashion outcomes of purpose and promise. Don't take these times lightly. Don't despise them either. *God is at work.* It reminds me of an often-quoted verse from the half brother of Jesus, James. Read James 1:2-4 (NIV) below:

"Consider it pure joy, my brothers, whenever you face trials of many kinds, because you know that the testing of your faith develops perseverance. Perseverance must finish its work so that you may be mature and complete, not lacking anything."

Would you be willing to view your current struggles with a new set of eyes? Would you be open to thinking differently about your marital hurdles? Do you have it in you to embrace your special needs child with a fresh compassion and involvement? Could the job you possess really be God's plan for your life in this season, even though it brings with it stress, frustration, and doubt? Never let go of God's exactness in your life needs. *He does not make mistakes.* God is working His miracles for your good. *Promotion is on the horizon.* Just over the hill. Around the next bend. Through the next door. Trust God, even when you can't trace His Hand. *Upgrade is coming!*

It's Your Move!

I. Have you ever had a turn around with new information?

    _____.

    How so? _____.

    _____.

2. Can you identify with the King of Babylon?

    _____.

    Are you a "See it to believe it" kind of person? _____.
    What makes you so? _____.

    _____.

3. What makes character so important? _____.
    Why do trials help to produce it? _____.

    _____.

4. *Promoted.* Rach, Shach, and Benny were elevated. Do you
    understand how? _____

    _____.

24

The Charge

This book took several years for me to write. Crazy, I know! As a new author, I didn't know the formula for completion. I would write a while, get all excited, and then life would put the brakes on. Time would pass. It always does. Then, someone would ask me how my book is coming. Feeling a bit embarrassed, I would have to confess that I had not worked on it in a while. Then, Christmas of 2016, my sweet daughter gave me a shadow box to put my first copy of my book in as a memorial of God's faithfulness in writing it through me. Guess what? I'm still not done. Close, but not done, even now in 2019. Funny how life works like that. Start. Stop. Start. Stop. Start. Stop. I lament.

If I had to guess, your life works like that too. We want to live in the IDEAL and we set out to make changes on the REAL, but then something happens to thwart our progress. Well, you are in good company. This *frustration* is the exact reason why I wrote the book in the first place. We start a lot of things. Admit it. We do. Get that off your chest. Throw it out into the middle of the room to view like a circus elephant. Floppy ears. Big butt. Large feet. Just hope it doesn't relieve itself in your living room. *Big Elephants* are hard to miss. They are also hard to get rid off, too. However, God is more interested in your progress than your pace, as noted earlier. Don't get lost in the worry of fast. Progress is key. Slow? That's OK. Unpredictable? Most of the time it is. March on, anyway. Work on getting the elephant out of your room and eventually out of your life. Confronting the Life Theme: *Expectations vs. Reality* is never easy. However, it is beneficial for your promotion.

God's plans for your life are good and working for you in spite of every fiery furnace you are facing today. No worries. Press into God. He is present. He is active. He is GOD. This last portion is the chorus by Jason Crabb, professional singer, who visits our church, Free Chapel, in Gainesville, GA often. He sang this song last Sunday (near Christmas in 2016) and it really touched me. It fits our theme well. Could it be that God fully knows the fires you walk through, daily? He does! These words echo a heart who has learned some things about the Christian faith and the God who represents it. Lean into the chorus of this incredible song by Jason Crabb.

~ Through the Fire ~

He never promised that the cross would not get heavy
And the hill would not be hard to climb
He never offered our victories without fighting
But He said help would always come in time
So just remember when you're standing in the valley of decision
And the adversary says give in
Just hold on, our Lord will show up
And He will take you through the fire again

As we close our time together, Fire is working in you as well as working around you. Fire is freeing you for the *Life* you long to live. Fire is your *Friend*. Take a few minutes to commit to memory this last verse from Isaiah 43: 2, (NIV):

> *When you pass through the waters,*
> *I will be with you;*
> *and when you pass through the rivers,*
> *they will not sweep over you.*
> *When you walk through the fire,*
> *you will not be burned;*
> *the flames will not set you ablaze.*

Wow! You made it to the end of the book. That calls for a personal celebration. Few readers make it to the last pages. Yes, many a book get a blast of energy at the beginning. Highlighted, underlined, pages folded for marking places, and xeroxed for retention. But, the back of the book gets little "loving". We tend to make sport of take-offs. However, landing the plane on a topic is usually less-than-common. Why? We run out of gas on our desire to create "Lasting Life Change"! Persistence takes the wind out of our "proverbial sails". Don't let this happen to you. You've come to far to *stall* out now. The BEST is still to come.

It's Your Move!

As a summary of all of the nine truths, please see the list below (cutout and carry with you for remembrance):

1. Fiery trials are <u>PART</u> of everyday <u>LIFE</u>.
2. Fiery trials get the whole world <u>LOOKING</u> at you.
3. Fiery trials <u>FORCE</u> you to choose sides. Do you believe in God or will you yield to the idols of the world?
4. Fiery trials <u>Bring out the Fight</u> for what is right regardless if you will lose everything in the process.
5. Fiery trials do not cause <u>FEAR</u> or <u>INTIMIDATION</u> for the "SECURE" Christian.
6. Fiery trials <u>CONSUME</u> the unbeliever, yet <u>CONFORMS</u> the Believer.
7. Fiery trials <u>BURN UP</u> the bands the <u>WORLD</u> places upon you.
8. Fiery trials give Jesus Christ the <u>OPPORTUNITY</u> to <u>JOIN</u> you in the fire.
9. Fiery trials produce <u>CHARACTER</u> conducive for <u>PROMOTION</u>.

~ <u>Your</u> *Personal Reflections* ~

[20] But as for you, you meant evil against me; *but* God meant it for good, in order to bring it about as *it is* this day, to save many people alive. Genesis 50:20 (NKJV)

Do you now believe this to be true? Why or why not?

~ <u>Your</u> *Personal Reflections* ~

Trust in the LORD with all your heart, and lean not on your own understanding; [6] In all your ways acknowledge Him, And He shall direct your paths. Proverbs 3:5-6 (NKJV)

Are you ready to let Him direct your steps? Yes? Why?

~ <u>Your</u> *Key Thoughts* ~

~ <u>Your</u> *Action Steps* ~

25

How to Know Jesus Christ, personally

Much attention was given in years past to shows like Extreme Makeover and Swan. The word *Makeover* became a household item. With each show, we were drawn in and fascinated by the before and after results. In fact, we were so intrigued by the transformation that we too wish we could be different. If we were honest, we each have a secret ambition to have something changed about ourselves. We may not verbalize it publicly, but it is there none the less. Sadly though, these are only external changes and *will not* lead to the <u>real</u> need in *your* life...A Makeover of the Heart! *Guess What? God had you in mind for such a Makeover. He calls it a Supreme Makeover!*

Why? ... God Loves You!

When sin entered into the world by Adam and Eve, the whole world was thrown into complete chaos, literally. The human race was in a *real* mess...physically, mentally, emotionally, spiritually, and relationally.

Physically - Mankind would now begin to feel the effects of physical deterioration

Mentally - Mankind would no longer pursue the mind and thoughts of God

Emotionally - Mankind was now afraid of God and hid himself from Him, alienated and alone.

Spiritually - Mankind was now separated from His Creator thus breaking intimate fellowship with Him

Relationally - Man and Woman were now in "opposition" with each other causing hurt, anger, isolation and loneliness

As you can see, we needed a *Divine* solution to <u>our</u> desperate dilemma - *Jesus Christ Came for you...*

1. Jesus Christ came to *"Revive"* you - *Physically*
2. Jesus Christ came to *"Renew"* you - *Mentally*
3. Jesus Christ came to *"Restore"* you - *Emotionally*
4. Jesus Christ came to *"Rescue"* you - *Spiritually*
5. Jesus Christ came to *"Rebuild"* you - *Relationally*

If all Jesus Christ came to do was to give you a once over spiritually, you might think "I don't need that now". Maybe, you might even say "When I get older, I'll consider spiritual matters". However, Jesus Christ came to give you a *Supreme Makeover* to be able to function in this present life and in the age to come, Eternal Life. <u>*Doesn't this sound AWESOME!*</u>

In all probability, you will be alive tomorrow and death will not be knocking at your door. However, *Real Life* causes you to need Jesus

Christ, *today*, as Savior and Master. Why go through life *incomplete* any longer! *It is time to consider what God has to offer you?*

Jesus Christ is *more* than a Savior. He is the *one* who wants to put your life back together, completely. Please don't deny His offer for <u>wholeness</u>. Your life depends on it. Maybe, your spouse is depending on this. Or, even your children! In fact, your eternal future depends on it!

Simply Pray:

Dear God,

I realize today that I am incomplete and broken by sin. The effects of sin have caused my life to be alienated and far from you. I have drifted along without purpose and joy for way too long. Today, I surrender my heart fully and sincerely to your Son, Jesus Christ. I invite Him into my life to give me a Supreme Makeover...physically, mentally, emotionally, spiritually, and relationally. I endeavor to make Him <u>first</u> priority in my life from this day forward. Thank you for giving me <u>new</u> life and an <u>abundant</u> life. In Jesus Christ's name I pray and believe. Amen.

Congratulations...You are a new creation!

Now we look inside, and what we see is that anyone united with the Messiah gets a <u>fresh start, is created new</u>. The old life is gone; a new life begins! Look at it! All this comes from the God who settled the relationship between us and him, and then called us to settle our relationships with each other. *2 Corinthians 5:17-18 (The Message)*

If you have prayed to receive Jesus Christ personally as Savior and Lord, please email me so

I can pray for you! (<u>WayMakerMinistriesInc@</u> <u>gmail.com</u>).

For Eternity's Sake,

Marvin Robert (a.k.a. "Bud")

Marvin Robert Wohlhueter, MA, Th.D., CLC

It's Your Move

About the Author

Marvin Robert Wohlhueter, MA, Th.D., CLC has a passion to partner with individuals to create the life they've dreamed of living. Through the coaching process, Marvin Robert seeks to encourage, equip, and empower individuals with tools for visionary living, defining priorities, goal setting, strategic thinking, and purpose-filled living. His step-by-step approach helps his clients to succeed in building successful futures, continued personal growth dynamics, and helps individuals to foster a passion for the life they want to live and thrive in, especially in their marital landscape and relational story.

Marvin Robert holds a Bachelor's degree in Mechanical Engineering and an Associates in Marketing Management. In addition, he has earned a Masters and Doctorate in Theology. Lastly, Marvin Robert has a Masters of Arts in Executive Leadership from Liberty University, earned in 2018. In October 2012, he obtained his certification as a Certified Life Coach from the Life Coaching Institute of Orange County in California. Marvin Robert and Lorraine live in Buford, Georgia (metro Atlanta area) where together they are building a healthy step-family with His two children, Raleigh and Jake. Also, they have twins (a boy and a girl) on the way due in early September, 2019. This is a celebration of God's faithfulness after years of believing to start a family.

Marvin Robert is the President & Founder of Way-Maker Ministries, Inc. in Atlanta, Ga. It was founded in 2018. Way-Maker Ministries, Inc. consists of seven distinct ingredients: Way-Maker Men (done on weekends), Way-Maker Women (done one weekends), Way-Maker Marriages (done one weekends), Way-Maker Life Coaching (done throughout the week), Way-Maker Worship, The Way-Maker Gathering (done on weekends) as well as Way-Maker Missions (done globally). Each area seeks to draw individuals into a personal relationship with God through His Son, Jesus Christ. To learn more visit: www.waymakerministry.com

To have Marvin Robert come speak for your next corporate, non-profit, civic, social, or private event (weekends only), please contact him at (678) 926-8990 or email him at waymakerministriesinc@gmail.com or visit his booking site @ www.marvinrobert.com. He would be honored to help your team, people, or congregation grow and thrive in life.

CPSIA information can be obtained
at www.ICGtesting.com
Printed in the USA
BVHW081823020919
557355BV00003B/245/P

9 781973 669067